W9-AHH-098

THE WORKING LIFE

A Medieval
Merchant

Titles in The Working Life series include:

THE WORKING LIFE

A Medieval Merchant

STUART A. KALLEN

LUCENT BOOKS

An imprint of Thomson Gale, a part of The Thomson Corporation

THOMSON
™
GALE

Detroit • New York • San Francisco • San Diego • New Haven, Conn. • Waterville, Maine • London • Munich

THOMSON
*
™
GALE

© 2005 Thomson Gale, a part of The Thomson Corporation.

Thomson and Star Logo are trademarks and Gale and Lucent Books are registered trademarks used herein under license.

For more information, contact
Lucent Books
27500 Drake Rd.
Farmington Hills, MI 48331-3535
Or you can visit our Internet site at http://www.gale.com

LIBRARY OF CONGRESS CATALOGING-IN-PUBLICATION DATA

Kallen, Stuart A., 1955–
    A medieval merchant / by Stuart Kallen.
        p. cm. — (The working life series)
    Includes bibliographical references and index.
    ISBN 1-59018-581-1 (hard cover : alk. paper)
    1. Merchants—Europe—History—To 1500—Juvenile literature. 2. Commerce—
History—Medieval, 500–1500—Juvenile literature. 3. Civilization, Medieval—
Juvenile literature. I. Title. II. Series.
    HF395.K35 2005
    381'.094'0902—dc22
                                                                    2004017471

Printed in the United States of America

CONTENTS

FOREWORD

"The strongest bond of human sympathy outside the family relations should be one uniting all working people of all nations and tongues and kindreds."

Abraham Lincoln, 1864

Work is a common activity in which almost all people engage. It is probably the most universal of human experiences. As Henry Ford, inventor of the Model T said, "There will never be a system invented which will do away with the necessity of work." For many people, work takes up most of their day. They spend more time with their coworkers than with family and friends. And the common goals people pursue on the job may be among the first thoughts that they have in the morning, and the last that they may have at night.

While the idea of work is universal, the way it is done and who performs it vary considerably throughout history. The story of work is inextricably tied to the history of technology, the history of culture, and the history of gender and race. When the typewriter was invented, for example, it was considered the exclusive domain of men who worked as secretaries. As women workers became more accepted, the secretarial role was gradually filled by women. Finally, with the invention of the computer, the modern secretary spends little time actually typing correspondence. Files are delivered via computer, and more time is spent on other tasks than the manual typing of correspondence and business.

This is just one example of how work brings together technology, gender, and culture. Another example is the American plantation slave. The harvesting of cotton was initially so cumbersome and time consuming that even with slaves its profitability was doubtful. With the invention of the cotton gin, however, efficiency improved, and slavery became a viable agricultural tool. It also became a southern tradition and institution, enough that the South was willing to go to war to preserve it.

The books in Lucent's Working Life series strive to show the intermingling of work, and its reflection in culture, technology, race, and gender. Indeed, history viewed through the perspective of the average worker is both enlightening and fascinating. Take the history of the typewriter, mentioned above. Readers today have access to more technology than any of their historical counterparts, and, in fact, though they would find the typewriter's keyboard familiar, they would find using it a bore. Finding out that people spent their days sitting over that machine (with no talk of carpal tunnel syndrome!) and were valued if they made no typing errors because corrections were cumbersome to make and, in some legal professions, made documents invalid, is an interesting story that involves many different aspects of history.

The desire to work is almost innate. As German socialist Ferdinand Lassalle said in the 1850s, "Workingmen we all are so far as we have the desire to make ourselves useful to human society in any way whatever." Yet each historical period offers a million different stories of the history of each job and how it was performed. And that history is the history of human society.

Each book in the Working Life series strives to tell the tale of these anonymous workers. Primary source quotes offer veracity and immediacy to each volume, letting the workers themselves tell their stories. In addition, thorough bibliographies tell students where they can find out more information, and complete indexes allow for easy perusal of the text. While students learn about the work of years gone by, they gain empathy for those who toil and, perhaps, a universal pride in taking up the work that will someday be theirs.

THE RISE OF THE MERCHANT CLASS

The ten centuries between the fifth century A.D. and the late 1400s are known as the medieval period, or the Middle Ages, a millennium bracketed by the fall of the Roman Empire and the great flowering of science and culture known as the Renaissance. The end of Roman authority meant the end of stable, safe conditions of trade and production, and the breakdown of social and economic links and infrastructure. Central government gave way to local rule, a confusion of tax and law codes, and the general fragmentation of European society.

MEDIEVAL DEMOGRAPHICS

Though change is inevitable in any period lasting ten centuries, some features of the Middle Ages were remarkably consistent. For example, the major cities on the European continent remained incredibly small by modern standards. In the fourteenth century, Paris—one of Europe's largest cities—had fewer than 80,000 people, compared with 8.7 million today. In fact, the entire population of Europe was an estimated 70 million, 15 million less than the number of people living in modern-day Germany. Cities for the most part were very unpleasant places, according to Gerhard Rempel:

> [Medieval towns] were noisy and dirty. . . . Filth, bad smells, and fires were constant hazards. Houses were built of combustible materials, open lamps and candles were used, and water was hard to command in the right spot. Rapid growth meant overcrowding, and overcrowding aggravated problems and dangers.
>
> Florence [in present-day Italy] did have public baths, sewers, and garbage collectors. However, in

many towns garbage was thrown in the gutter along with human excrement and urine. Plumbing was primitive or non-existent. Butchers slaughtered animals within the city limits. Without the means of refrigeration, fish and meat became stinking and putrid. Houses, to save space, were sometimes built out over the streets. Thus they cut off light and air for passers-by and even endangered horsemen's heads. [1]

These unsanitary conditions fostered the spread of disease and allowed the Black Plague, carried by flea-infested rats, to ravage Europe soon after it first appeared in 1347. It reappeared about every twenty years or so

MEDIEVAL EUROPE

for the rest of the Middle Ages. The initial epidemic killed over 20 million people, about one-third of the European population. Those who survived disease were nonetheless plagued by wars, which were also nearly constant throughout the era.

Constant strife did not threaten the rigid and durable social structure of the Middle Ages. The peasantry composed 80 to 90 percent of the population. This vast lower class was controlled by small ruling elites consisting of the nobility—local lords and their

Skeletons representing the Black Plague claim their victims in this medieval woodcut.

vassals such as knights and barons—and Christian religious leaders. Collectively the nobility, clergy, and peasants were known as the divinely ordained orders. In this strict social hierarchy, each order had its own role as predetermined by God. The nobility owned the land, collected taxes, and oversaw defenses on their tiny independent estates, known as fiefdoms. The church not only was the ultimate authority on spiritual matters but also guided the practices and duties of daily life. The peasants farmed the land, produced the food, and otherwise supported the church and nobility.

EARLY MERCHANTS

In general, there was little money in circulation, and most commodities not produced on individual fiefdoms were obtained by barter in small market towns. Crafts people who made farm implements, dishes, clothing, and other items were usually paid for their efforts in grain, wine, meat, textiles, or the free use of a small piece of farmland.

One group of people did not fit into the divine order. Beginning around the tenth century, peddlers began traveling from town to town to supply peasants and nobility alike with the necessary wares of daily life. A few of the common items offered by one seller were described by twelfth-century English writer John of Garland:

William . . . has in the market these things before him to be sold: needles and needlecases, cleansing material or soap, mirrors, razors, whetstones . . . fire-striking irons, and spindles. . . . Barons, be patient, the most expensive things are coming last . . . among the first are inks, sulpher, incense, quicksilver, alum, [dye], peppers, saffron, furs, tanned leather, shoe leather, and marten skins.[2]

William's offerings were humble but in great demand; no doubt a crowd of eager shoppers examined his goods.

The fact that William was able to travel from town to town is, in itself, a testament to the rising importance of merchants. Before the tenth century, the larger medieval villages were mostly religious and military centers that barely developed beyond serving the most basic needs of the officials or soldiers who lived there. When traveling merchants began to frequent central areas, however, towns quickly developed as they attracted people from the surrounding area. Robert S. Lopez and Irving W. Raymond explain this phenomenon in *Medieval Trade in the Mediterranean World:*

A town . . . by its very existence stimulates trade and manufacture. It brings together a number of consumers who need food and other necessities that they cannot produce. . . . Medieval towns . . . played a greater role in commercial development because an ever-growing proportion of the population was made up of . . . merchants.[3]

DEVELOPING MODERN BUSINESS PRACTICES

As trading centers grew into large towns, the quality of the wares provided by merchants improved significantly in the twelfth century. At that time, favorable political alliances allowed trade routes to open up between the Middle East, North Africa, and Italian cities such as Pisa, Genoa, and Venice. The nobility prospered and could afford to demand gems, silks, exotic spices, and other symbols of wealth and status originating in distant realms. The itinerant merchant, who once simply wandered from town to town, increasingly was required to travel by ship to Turkey, Morocco, Egypt, Syria, and other foreign locations.

This expansion of trade and commerce added considerable complexity to the merchant business. At the most basic level, purchasing goods required the minting of gold, silver, or copper coins by a wide variety of kings, nobles, and local officials. That meant the merchant needed to understand the complex exchange rate—for example, between the French denier,

This thirteenth-century drawing shows medieval merchants using a camel to transport goods to a ship waiting to sail to distant ports.

the Genoese florin, and the Greek tournois. To further complicate matters, coinage was often in short supply, forcing merchants to accept payment in such diverse forms as squirrel skins or wine.

Trading large quantities of goods over great distances also required the merchant to enter into risky business ventures with a large assortment of others, including shippers, sailors, translators, and longshoremen who were needed to move the goods to market. The expenses incurred during such transactions often forced merchants to enter into business ventures with other merchants in order to pool money and resources. These joint partnerships required an understanding of contracts, banking, bills of exchange, credit, accounting, and other complicated issues of commerce.

CHANGING THE FACE OF SOCIETY

In this world of trade and commerce, every merchant faced a multitude of risks. Ships laden with goods sank at sea or were hijacked by pirates. Primitive rutted roads broke the axles of wagons and the legs of horses, and the surrounding forests were filled with bandits. The market was fickle, with sudden gluts or shortages of goods caused by public whims. Wars, epidemics, and social upheavals could ruin a merchant overnight—or even end his life. Merchants also needed the consent of nobility and clergy to operate, and obtaining permissions was often expensive and time-consuming. And finally, though people desired imported goods, merchants were long accorded a very low status and considered avaricious parasites. This attitude is explained in "Medieval Merchant Culture":

> The merchant, as a class, was discriminated against for not contributing to [the three divinely ordained orders], but rather for aiming to get rich himself. His pursuit of gain was considered against the laws of God, because he was not a producer of real goods, but rather a resaler, or a usurer. Although medieval society increasingly came to rely upon the merchant's services in distributing and obtaining items

The medieval city of Venice bustled with mercantile activity as ships laden with goods from across the known world sailed along its canals.

not produced locally, he was none-theless considered a parasite and a sinner, barely tolerated for his questionable contribution to society's output. [4]

Despite these attitudes, the activities of the traders permanently changed the face of European society in what has been called the commercial revolution. As the centuries passed, the center of power shifted from the land-holdings of the nobility to the merchant's world of banks and commerce. The concentration of wealth in cities such as Florence, Venice, Paris, and London attracted people, eager to get rich, from all over the world. The need for stability and protection of assets meant that merchants used their money and power to support kings and the establishment of strong central governments. Prosperous joint-venture companies employed thousands of people, many of whom would have otherwise been impoverished peasants in the divinely ordained orders.

Until the rise of the merchant class, only people born into the nobility had access to such privileges as fine art, exotic foods and other luxuries, and large estates. The merchant's wealth gained him entry into high society for the first time. By the time the Renaissance period ended the Middle Ages in the sixteenth century, some merchants were famous patrons of the arts, building concert halls, churches, and other cultural amenities.

While often overlooked in the grand sweep of history, medieval merchants brought wealth and culture to the masses. And in doing so they created a society in which even a lowly peasant could rise to the level of a knight or prince through hard work, study, and aptitude, and helped dissolve a social structure that had defined European civilization for a thousand years.

CHAPTER 1

TRAVELING THE TRADE ROUTES

During the medieval era, peasants worked from dawn to dusk, and few ever traveled more than a day's walk from where they were born. While these farmers toiled ceaselessly, the nobles spent most of their time on their estates feasting, hunting, and engaging in other pleasurable pursuits. They traveled more than peasants, visiting other nobles or raising armies to fight regional wars, but their knowledge of other cultures was usually limited. The main contact that these people, rich and poor, had with the wider world was through trade goods brought to their towns by merchants who traveled the world to conduct business.

By the tenth century, medieval trade routes were extensive, connecting Britain, the European continent, the Middle East, and North Africa by river and by sea. Throughout the Middle East and Asia were some excellent overland trade routes, although the passable roads in Europe were few.

In the northern countries, coal, wool, and tin flowed between England and Scandinavia. Citrus fruits, leather, and barrels of honey were transported from present-day Spain and Portugal north to Stockholm, Leipzig, and Moscow. The northern woods of present-day Russia provided fish, furs, timber, and grain to the rest of the Mediterranean trading region. Human slaves were bought in Slavic countries and shipped to southern Europe. High-quality swords and armor were shipped from Toledo, Spain, to the Levant countries of Egypt, Israel, Lebanon, Syria, and Turkey, on the eastern shore of the Mediterranean. From the Middle East, India, and China, spices, glassware, ceramics, carpets, ivory, and gems traveled by camel, ox, and ship to ports in Rome, Venice, and Florence where olive oil, wine, glassworks, and

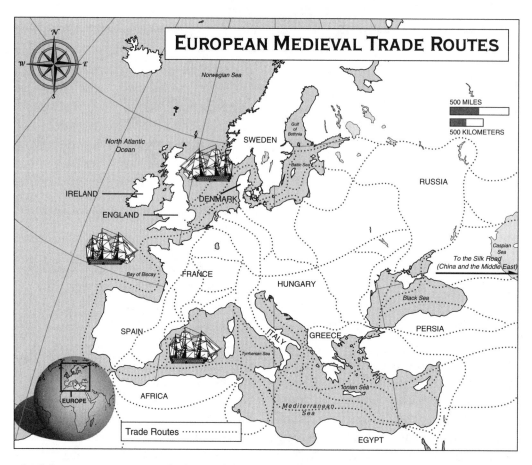

EUROPEAN MEDIEVAL TRADE ROUTES

Norwegian Sea

500 MILES

500 KILOMETERS

SWEDEN

Gulf of Bothnia

Baltic Sea

RUSSIA

North Atlantic Ocean

IRELAND

DENMARK

ENGLAND

Caspian Sea

To the Silk Road (China and the Middle East)

Bay of Biscay

FRANCE

HUNGARY

Black Sea

SPAIN

ITALY

GREECE

PERSIA

Tyrrhenian Sea

EUROPE

AFRICA

Ionian Sea

Mediterranean Sea

Trade Routes

EGYPT

clothing were exported throughout Europe.

LIFE ON THE SILK ROAD

While hundreds of items were bought and sold within the Mediterranean region, the products most valuable to the merchant—and his customers— came from China, a region then called Cathay. Chinese goods such as silks, spices, ceramic dishes and vases, gunpowder, jade, bronze objects, and iron were carried to the ports in the Levant along a series of east-west routes

known collectively as the Silk Road. This four-thousand-mile-long web of ancient paths was first developed around the second century B.C. Three main routes led out of the present-day city of Xi'an, China, and hundreds of smaller paths connected villages and towns along the way. The northern route ran westward from China to the Black Sea in eastern Europe; the central route passed through Persia (present-day Iraq and Iran) and ended in Rome, Italy, via the Mediterranean Sea. The southern route of the

Silk Road connected Afghanistan, Iran, and India.

Medieval merchants hauled their products along the Silk Road using caravans that consisted of anywhere from one hundred to one thousand camels, each loaded with roughly five hundred pounds of goods. Some routes along the Silk Road were well developed, policed, and free from bandits. Other parts of the route were extremely dangerous, however, and merchants were forced to incur the added expense of hiring defense forces to protect their goods.

Numerous other perils haunted merchants along the Silk Road. Some were lost in harsh desert sandstorms, while others froze to death on high mountain passes. Sometimes routes were impassable because of weather, wars, or robber gangs, and merchants lost valuable time and energy taking longer routes. With all these problems, only the most valuable cargoes warranted the risks inherent in transporting them to Europe.

To minimize the medieval merchant's troubles, Francesco di Balduccio Pegolotti wrote a handbook

A fifteenth-century painting shows merchants conversing as goods are unloaded from their ships. Medieval merchants captivated listeners with stories of the world beyond Europe.

around 1310 called *The Road to China: A Merchant's Guide.* The book described things merchants should know when traveling the western portions of the Silk Road:

> First of all, it is advisable for him to let his beard grow long and not shave. And at Tana (Madagascar) he should furnish himself with dragomans [translators] and he should not try to save by hiring a poor one instead of a good one, since a good one does not cost [much more]. . . . And besides dragomans he ought to take along at least two good menservants who know the Cumanic [Turkish] tongue well. . . . And [for the stretch] from Tana to Astrakhan [Russia] he ought to furnish himself with food for twenty-five days—that is, with flour and salt fish, for you find meat in sufficiency in every locality along the road. And in like manner, to the aforesaid [number of] days, you ought to furnish yourself with flour and salt fish; for other things you find in sufficiency, and especially meat.[5]

THE MERCHANT MOTEL AND TRADE CENTER

Life was difficult for traveling merchants, but there were places along the way where they could rest, make deals, and take care of other necessities. Those traveling to Islamic cities such as Alexandria, Damascus, and Tunis encountered large two-story facilities, called *funduqs,* that rented out as many as one hundred rooms. At these medieval motels, part inn and part business center, merchants lodged, dined, bathed, stabled their horses, purchased goods from local crafts-

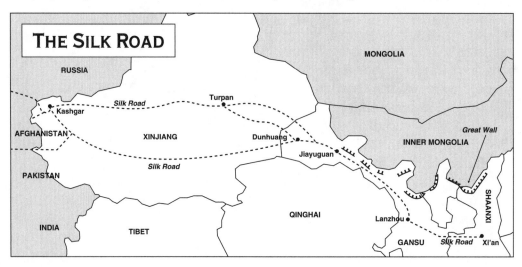

THE SILK ROAD

MONGOLIA
RUSSIA
Silk Road
Turpan
Kashgar
AFGHANISTAN
XINJIANG
Dunhuang
Great Wall
INNER MONGOLIA
Jiayuguan
Silk Road
PAKISTAN
SHAANXI
INDIA
TIBET
QINGHAI
Lanzhou
GANSU
Silk Road
Xi'an

TIGERS, EUNUCHS, OSTRICHES, AND TROTTING DONKEYS

In the mid–ninth century, royal emissary Ibn Fadlan traveled the medieval trade routes, purchasing items in various towns for shipment to Iraq. He kept a detailed list of these trade goods, which included everything from Indian panthers to Chinese saddles to Iranian dancing girls. Fadlan's list is reprinted in Medieval Trade in the Mediterranean World, *edited by Robert S. Lopez and Irving W. Raymond:*

From India are imported tigers, panthers, elephants, panther skins, rubies, white sandal, ebony, and coconuts.

    From China are imported silk stuffs . . . peacocks, racing horses, saddles, felts, cinnamon, Greek unblended rhubarb. [Also] are imported utensils of gold and silver . . . dinars [coins] of pure gold, drugs, brocades, racing horses, female slaves, knicknacks with human figures, . . . hydraulic engineers, expert agronomists, marble workers, and eunuchs. . . .

    From Egypt: trotting donkeys, suits of fine cloth, papyrus, balsam, and from its mines—topazes of superior quality.

    From the land of the Khazars [present-day Ukraine]: slaves of both sexes, coats of mail, [and] helmets. . . .

    From Merv [in Central Asia]: zither players [and] valuable zithers. . . .

    From Ahwaz [central Iran]: . . . castanets [and] dancing girls.

---

people, converted their money to regional currency, paid local taxes, obtained necessary trading permits, and held business meetings. Most important, *funduqs* provided secured facilities where merchants could store their valuable wares. In the twelfth century, Spanish Muslim author Ibn Jubayr described the secured rooms of *funduqs* as built "like a fortress in their unassailableness and their fortifications. Their doors are of iron, and they present the greatest strength."[6]

On the second floor, above the storerooms, were guest rooms that featured balconies with wooden railings. Individual merchants could rent private rooms or share spaces with as many as ten people. During the extremely hot desert summer, most slept on the roofs of the *funduqs* to enjoy the night breeze. In 1326, Arab trader Ibn Batuta described how he spent a night in a *funduq* in Rosetta, Egypt: "[My host advised that I] go up on the roof . . . and sleep there, for this was during the summer heats . . . so I ascended to the roof and found there a straw mattress and a leather mat, vessels for ritual ablutions, a jar of water and a drinking cup, and I lay down there to sleep."[7]

Although these *funduqs* were ubiquitous in many Arab trading cities, they were not open to the public. Rather, they were places where merchants, importers, and manufacturers of goods could live, mingle, and conduct business. Within the *funduqs* merchants could practice their Christian or Jewish faiths, follow their European customs, and drink alcohol where it was otherwise forbidden because of Muslim beliefs. However, the European guests were locked in the *funduqs* at night so they would not influence or corrupt the local people.

A MULTICULTURAL BUSINESS

The *funduqs* were cross-cultural centers where medieval trade was conducted between European, Arab, Indian, and Asian traders. At a time when most peasants rarely met anyone whose beliefs or practices differed from their own, the world of merchants was a cornucopia of multiculturalism. Doing business required merchants to speak many languages and trade a wide variety of goods, a point made in a description of the travels of Jewish merchants written around 886 by an Arab trader, Abu al-Qasim:

These merchants speak Arabic, Persian, Roman [Latin], Frankish [French], Spanish, and Slavonic. They travel from the East to the West and from the West to the East by land as well as by sea. They bring from the West eunuchs, slave girls, boys, [silks], beaver skins, marten furs, and other varieties of furs, and swords. They embark in the land of the Franks [present-day France] on the Western Sea [Mediterranean], and they sail towards al-Farama [in Egypt]. There they load their merchandise on the backs of camels and proceed by land to al-Qulzum [on the Nile delta]. . . .

They embark on the Eastern Sea [Indian Ocean] and proceed . . . [to] China. On their return from China they load musk, aloe, wood, camphor, cinnamon, and other products of the eastern countries and they come back to al-Qulzum . . . and from there they embark again on the Western Sea. Some of them sail for Constantinople in order to sell their merchandise to the Romans. Others proceed to the residence of the king of the Franks to dispose of their articles. [8]

STORMS, PIRATES, AND SEA TRADING

Such traders were well acquainted with the formidable difficulty of transporting goods on medieval trade routes, which was costly and complicated. Until the twelfth century, large sailing ships to move merchandise did not exist. During this period, merchants moved goods on the Mediterranean, Baltic, and North seas in rowboats manned by up to ninety rowers, with three men assigned to each oar. These large crews were problematic, however, as the weight of the men, plus their food and water, exceeded the weight of the cargo that the boat would hold.

Around the eleventh century, ships with sails were developed that could move large quantities of wheat, salt, wine, red herring, wool, wood, and other bulky cargoes. While rowboats had to stay close to shore, the ships expanded trade routes by sailing across open ocean. During this time, many merchants became expert sailors as well. Speaking of Godric, an eleventh-century English merchant, Joseph Gies and Frances Gies write in *Merchants and Moneymen:*

> Godric was not a mere passenger on the ships that carried his merchandise; he took part in the operation of the vessel, and became an expert mariner, serving sometimes as navigator, sometimes as pilot. Eventually he became ship's master. He studied winds, currents,

Throughout the Middle Ages, magnificent ships like this one were designed to transport large quantities of goods over great distances.

and weather as carefully as merchandise and market conditions. . . . Without the aid of compass or astrolabe [navigational tools that had not yet been invented] he found his course by the sun and stars.[9]

While Godric may have been an expert navigator, sailing ships carried great risks. They could get blown off course, driven onto rocks, or stranded in doldrums when no winds blew. Rough seas and storms were also an ever-present problem. Merchant Robert Bargrave traveled extensively by ship during the seventeenth century. Although he did not work in the medieval period, his experiences of sailing from England to Constantinople show that similar business trips carried considerable risks, judging from his entry in *The Travel Diary of Robert Bargrave, Levant Merchant:*

No sooner had we sett saile, but the wind grew exceeding boistrous. . . . We stood some [hours] Combat with the violent Tempest but the Wind turning at last directly against us, forc'd us to retreat: Neither could we escape thus the Fury of the Storme; which though it spared us to tell our own Story, yet [drowned] almost all our living Provisions upon the open Deck. . . . I found my selfe in a strange world, the Seae beating sometimes into my very Cabin; & I tossd & tumbled, sometimes my bed upon mee, & sometimes I upon my bed now on my head then on my heeles, all wett & dabled [splattered], sick, hungry without sleep, & in a confusion of Torments.[10]

With such dangers inherent in sea travel, valuable cargoes such as gems, silk, and spices that required less room continued to be moved by massive seagoing rowboats. The coast-hugging boats were able to go ashore during storms. They were also more maneuverable in case of problems and easier to defend in battle. As Jean Favier writes in *Gold and Spices: The Rise of Commerce in the Middle Ages:* "No other vessel could equal [the rowboat's] ability to outwit pirates . . . outstrip pursuers, or penetrate blockades."[11]

Merchants ensured that they were protected from pirates in other ways as well, often hiring a ship filled with mercenary soldiers to accompany their cargoes. When Italian merchant Francesco di Marco Datini shipped his wool, bales of cloth, and tin from Southampton, England, to Majorca, he wrote his partners that the "ship will be accompanied by 50 good men, furnished with arms and crossbows."[12]

The crossbowmen were simply part of doing business at a time when pirates would capture any unarmed ship they found. The privateers often

A Fourteenth-Century Merchant's Travel Guide

Around 1310, Italian author Francesco di Balduccio Pegolotti wrote a medieval handbook for merchants called The Practice of Commerce, *which provided invaluable information for merchants traveling to China along the Silk Road. The following excerpt, quoted in* The Records of Medieval Europe, *edited by Carolly Erickson, instructs the merchant on various means of travel and offers other advice:*

First [of all], from Tana to Astrakhan [Russia] it is twenty-five days by ox wagon, and from ten to twelve days by horse wagon. Along the road you meet many Mongolians, that is, armed men. . . .

And from [the Kazakstan cities of] Saraichuk to Urjench it is twenty days by camel wagon—and for those who are carrying wares it is convenient to go through Urjench, because that is a good market for wares—and from Urjench to Utrar it is from thirty-five to forty days by camel wagon. . . .

And from Utrar to Almaligh [Central Asia] it is forty-five days by pack asses. And you meet Mongolians every day. . . .

And from the river you can travel to Wuinsay [Hang-chow] and sell there any silver sommi [coins] you have, because that is a good market for wares. And from Quinsay on you travel with the money you get for the silver sommi you have sold there, that is, with paper money. And said money is called balisci, four of these are worth one silver sommi throughout the country of Cathay [China].

demanded huge ransoms from merchants for the return of their goods—and for the people on board.

With the dangers inherent in sea travel, merchants were the first people to lobby governments for laws to protect their trade. For example, the fourteenth-century Visby Sea Laws, enacted around the North and Baltic seas, covered a wide variety of regulations on many merchant concerns including the quality of ropes used in handling cargo, the handling of salvageable goods in case of shipwrecks, the responsibilities of captains, the settlement of disputes with sailors, and even the quantity of food given to crews. One example concerns drunkenness, which was a notorious problem among sailors:

Mariners [sailors] hire themselves out to their Master [the merchant] and some of them go ashore without leave and get drunk and make a disturbance and some be hurt.

The Master is not under obligation to have them healed. . . . He may put them ashore and hire others in their place. [13]

A WET AND MUDDY ROAD

Merchants' troubles did not end with the arrival of their goods at great seaports such as Venice, Bruges, Hamburg, and Barcelona. From these cities, merchants distributed goods throughout Europe using rivers and roads. Like the sea, these routes were fraught with risk and hardship. Roads were particularly troublesome because land was privately held by nobility. There were no county or provincial governments to build and maintain roads. Moreover, a good road was a bad thing to the nobility and peasants in small villages because it simply provided enemies easy access in case of attack. Under these circumstances, merchants faced tough traveling conditions, as Favier explains:

The merchant's road was, then, a simple path, sometimes hard and dusty in other cases muddy and wet. Although pitted with deep ruts, the road would otherwise be unmarked; the merchant could easily lose his way or sink into the marshy ground. Here the packhorse came into its own. Although it could carry little more than [several hundred pounds], such an animal could heave itself out of the mud and carry its pack of goods well out of the dust where its master walked. A wagon could carry more. These heavy four-wheeled vehicles traveled in convoys transporting heavy loads such as salt, wheat, stone, and wood. . . . It was not unusual to find wagons carrying one and a half tons; on the other hand a wagon that sticks in the mud represents a lost load, and a wagon team traveled slowly. The faster two-wheeled cart was fine in good weather for the merchant carrying goods over short distances. [14]

These conditions began to change in the thirteenth century when kings and princes went on an unprecedented road- and bridge-building binge in response to the growing political power of merchants and the public demand for more readily available merchandise.

BARGES, BOATS, AND TOLLS

The alternative to wagons and muddy paths was the barge and boat. Europe's many great rivers had been used for commercial activities for thousands of years. Central Europe was accessible through the Rhine, Rhone, Elbe, and Danube water systems. France has, among others, the Seine and the Loire, while England has the Thames. During the medieval era, towpaths lined parts of these waterways so men and mules could pull shallow-draft boats and rafts that were laden with merchandise.

Rivers presented a different set of problems to the merchant. Modern waterways are typically dredged and channeled for commercial ship traffic, but medieval rivers were mostly in their natural state. This prompted one unnamed bargeman to write of the Eure River in France: "The river is much encumbered with trees, reeds, grasses and very low in water,"[15] during the dry season. Rivers also often turned into raging torrents during rainy months, making them useless for transportation. In the winter, boats could be trapped and destroyed by ice floes.

Hazardous weather was always unpredictable; tolls and taxes, on the other hand, were a constant burden. Most major rivers were ruled by powerful knights who earned fortunes by controlling sections of the river traffic from huge castles constructed along the banks. Heavily armed soldiers stopped passing boats with chains or ropes and forced the merchants to pay exorbitant tolls. In the mid-1300s,

This fourteenth-century sketch shows men struggling as they transport goods up a hill. Transporting goods by land was very difficult in the Middle Ages.

there were fifty-one such toll stops on the Rhine, between present-day France and Germany, and thirty-one in France on the Garonne River alone. This added considerably to the cost of business for the merchant. By the 1500s, the cost of tolls was often about half the price the merchant paid for the products he was shipping.

River tolls were only part of the merchant's tax burden. The list of taxes, tolls, and fees incurred by Pegolotti when he transported wool from London to Florence is compiled by Edwin S. Hunt in *The Medieval Super-Companies:*

In London, customs and export tax had to be paid, along with tips to officials, wine for the clerks, fees to the customs weigher and broker, charges for porters, haulage, customs porters, and shipping to Libourne in Gascony, near Bordeaux. There the wool incurred

---

ꙮ THE IMPORTANCE OF SPICES ꙮ

During the medieval period, certain spices were as valuable as gold. In the Web article "The Influence of Spice Trade on the Age of Discovery," Patty Strassmann explains why:

The diet of the average European in the middle ages was bland at best. The lack of refrigeration and poor quality meats required some spices to make them edible. . . .

There were many spices that were popular with Europeans in the middle ages. Cinnamon came from China and Burma and was used not only for flavor but for cosmetics, drugs, balms, oils, and perfume. Nutmeg came from the Banda Islands [in Indonesia]. Cloves came from only two islands: Ternate and Tidore in the Moluccas (south of Indonesia) which were also known as the Spice Islands. Pepper was grown only in India . . . [and] was used ex-tensively in cooking but was also used for a tonic, a stimulant, even as insect repellent and an aphrodisiac. . . .

Spices were also used as a means of exchange. There was no international currency exchange at this time. All payments between countries were made in gold and silver. Spices could also be used to pay fines and mortgages, to buy land, to buy a coat of arms or to pay taxes. . . .

[During medieval times] the spices were transported on Italian ships to Venice and Genoa [and from there to the rest of Europe]. . . . The Italian merchants who sponsored these trade caravans became very wealthy and influential. The cost and risk was very high but the rewards were great. It was said that a merchant could ship six cargoes, and lose five, but still make a profit when the sixth was sold.

innkeeper charges for the personnel and temporary storage, carriage and turnpike fees for the overland trip from Libourne to Montpellier and then on to Aigues-Mortes, where it was transferred to the port and loaded on a ship for Pisa. In Italy there were porter, warehousing, carriage, and notarial fees to pay, followed by tolls at three different locations, unloading at Signa, carriage from Signa to Florence, and customs in Florence. Assuming all went well, the entire trip would take several months. . . . But often all did not go well. The many transfers and formalities afforded almost unlimited opportunities for delays. Ships that turned back to ports in England to escape piracy or bad weather were sometimes held up for customs examination all over again. On such occasions, the king had to intervene with letters of authentication to satisfy the officials that appropriate duties had already been paid.[16]

"MAN IS A DANGEROUS THING"

Taxes and tolls were minor frustrations compared with medieval merchants' daily dread of wars, revolutions, and robbers. As a sixty-two-year-old Datini wrote in 1397 to a young man just starting in the business, "When you have lived as long as I and have traded with many folks, you will know that man is a dangerous thing, and that danger lies in dealing with him."[17]

Traveling merchants were also away from home for years at a time. For example, Bargrave's journey from England to Constantinople and back took five years. Such was the life of merchants for whom business was a way of life. Bargrave's words likely sum up the feelings of many merchants upon returning home after long, dangerous journeys: "[Reverently] kissing my native [soil], I praise God for his inestimable kindness; through whose Protection I began my Journey so prosperously, perform'd it so safely, and finish'd it so successfully."[18]

CHAPTER 2

MERCHANTS AT MARKETS AND FAIRS

Medieval trade was conducted in a variety of ways. In the early Middle Ages, some merchants manufactured products such as clothing, eating utensils, jewelry, weapons, or tools at home and sold them from the windows of their houses. By the tenth century, weekly markets where merchants could sell their wares, and goods produced by others, had been established in thousands of villages and towns throughout Europe. Major cities also hosted annual or biannual fairs where merchants met to trade with one another. In all, these economic developments created a system of commerce that brought trade goods from across Europe and the Eastern world to the homes of peasants, nobility, and clergy alike.

THE PEDDLER AND HIS PACK

In many parts of rural Europe where villages were small, merchants were simply peddlers who loaded their goods on their backs and walked from one town to the next, often selling their products door-to-door. The eleventh-century written account of Godric provides a glimpse into the peddler's life. Godric was a strong, thickset man with a heavy black beard who began his career as a boy, scavenging along the Lincolnshire coast, hoping to find goods washed up from the all-too-common shipwrecks. On occasion, Godric found marketable items in the wreckage and sold them in town markets. By saving his meager profits, he was eventually able to buy a supply of cheap items such as needles, scissors, knives, and religious ribbons.

With a few days' supply of dried meat and biscuits, Godric walked through the countryside, stopping at farms along the way to make sales. Since money was scarce, Godric most often traded his items for food, wool, or other goods. Walking with sore feet through sleet, snow, and rain, Godric wrote hymns that he sang to keep his spirits up: "Christ and St. Mary support me . . . that I on this earth should not with my bare foot tread." [19]

By working hard and saving, Godric was soon able to acquire finer products such as herbal medicines, silver cups, metal utensils, and cloth. These he took to the large stone castles to show to the lords and ladies who lived there. Godric also made sales calls to the

The medieval peddler was a one-man market, carrying goods on his back and walking from town to town to conduct trade.

wealthy abbots and bishops who resided in monasteries and churches.

When not selling door-to-door, Godric was able to trade at local markets where foreign merchants brought exotic goods from the East. The Gieses describe the situation: "[There] great lords and members of the royal court came to buy furs, cloth, spices, and wine. Godric bought wholesale, to sell to his customers on the road." [20]

After leaving a market with his pack overflowing with goods, Godric traveled with other merchants, armed to fend off bandits. The deep woods between villages were particularly dangerous and only to be crossed during daylight hours. At night, Godric might trade his wares with a farmer for dinner, a night's lodging in a barn, and breakfast.

THE MEDIEVAL MARKET

In the eleventh century, the English markets that Godric patronized were sponsored by abbeys and churches. By the second half of the twelfth century, however, noblemen discovered they could make tidy profits by selling the rights to hold markets on property they controlled. To do so, plots of land were leased by town leaders. Local merchants were charged a small fee to sell their goods on one day of the week, often Friday. Merchants sold pottery, shoes, cloth, food, and other products from their dusty packs, two-wheeled carts, or covered stalls.

Although the stalls were supposed to be shut down at the end of the day, some stayed open all week long and were eventually turned into permanent buildings. Italian author Bonvesin della Riva provides an example of the scene at the Milan market in 1288:

> It is amazing to see almost innumerable merchants with their variety of wares and buyers flocking to all these [markets]. Furthermore . . . practically anything that a man may need is brought daily not only to [the markets] but even into the [open] squares, and all that can be sold is loudly advertised for sale. . . . [Every] week merchants and buyers hasten to . . . them in large numbers. It is evident . . . that in our city it is a wonderful life for those who have money enough. [21]

The network of weekly markets was one of the main components of the booming economic progress that swept across the region during the Middle Ages. These markets spurred the creation of money and monetary standards and brought modest wealth to thousands of merchants who either produced goods or resold products provided by importers.

EXTRAORDINARY CONFUSION

A typical market day began for most merchants around six o'clock in the

A fifteenth-century drawing shows the activity of a busy market. Medieval markets were packed with many merchants competing for the business of customers.

morning, after the first mass of the day had concluded. By 7:00 A.M., the market was teeming with people. The smells of freshly baked bread and exotic spices mingled with the stench of unrefrigerated meat, day-old fish, animal manure, and unwashed bodies.

Markets were noisy places where merchants yelled out offers, or were said to "cry the wares," as a way of advertising their products to passersby. The most enthusiastic merchants waded into crowds and forcibly pushed or pulled prospective customers over to their booths. Hundreds of animals

awaiting purchase or slaughter added to the cacophony, as twelfth-century Greek writer Lucian explains: "I was struck with wonder at the number and variety of the animals, and the extraordinary confusion of their noises which assailed my ears—horses neighing, oxen lowing, sheep bleating, pigs grunting, and dogs barking, for these also accompany their masters as a defense against wolves and thieves."²²

Things quieted down around 9:00 A.M., when people paused to eat breakfast. By ten o'clock traffic picked up again as shoppers searched through the

❧ WOMEN IN THE MEDIEVAL MARKET ❧

Women in England had few rights during the Middle Ages. For example, women were legally considered to be the property of their husbands. In the fourteenth century, however, participation of women in the marketplace allowed female merchants to attain an official legal status known as femme sole. *This term, which translated literally as "woman alone" or "single woman," referred to any woman who conducted business on her own, including married women who were merchants in the marketplace. This unique legal status is explained in the Web article "Introduction to Late Medieval English Mercantile Narratives and Gendered Mercantile Concerns":*

[Femme] sole status was to allow a woman to [preclude] the need for her spouse's participation and agreement in mercantile contracts. Femme sole status also allowed a wife to act as her husband's agent if he were not present. This status therefore granted wives significant power to act on their own, with or without their husbands, in both mercantile and legal realms, and as such it represents an extremely important historical moment in the history of women's power. . . .

The figure of the "medieval businesswoman" disrupted the traditional [gender roles] of the late Middle Ages, a system wherein practically all levels of society were male dominated. Women of the late fourteenth century, in part because of the development of femme sole status, found a position within the merchant classes through which they could exert a certain amount of social . . . and, ultimately, economic control.

wide variety of goods. Some sellers were farmers who acted as part-time merchants in order to sell their surplus grains, vegetables, fruit, eggs, meat, milk, and livestock. Others were bakers, brewers, potters, and candle makers who were producers, selling goods on market days that they manufactured in their homes. Fishmongers, people who caught and sold fish and seafood, were also commonly seen at weekly markets.

Medieval markets also provided a newfound sense of independence for women who, while barred from many jobs, were able to earn their own money as merchants. According to the Web article "Introduction to Late Medieval English Mercantile Narratives and Gendered Mercantile Concerns":

That women were a major part of the merchant constituency is undeniable. . . . [Records] show, for example, that . . . fourteenth- and fifteenth-century London women [were] active in trade and merchant activities as disparate as hucksters [peddlers], brokers, threadwomen, pouchmakers, mercers [silk and textile dealers] . . . book binders and sellers, jewelers, and even [armor makers]. Based on these references, women were a significant part of most medieval mercantile systems: buying and selling grain and livestock; investing in, purchasing, and selling real estate; dominating the victualing [food] and service trades; actively participating in transactions; and, of course, common figures in all textile trades, including the manufacture, distribution and resale of cloth.[23]

GAMES, ARTS, AND SWEARING

The medieval market was more than a place for women and men to sell products, however. It was also a center of social activity where visitors could eat prepared foods, drink wine and beer, and watch horse races, ball games, javelin-throwing contests, and

Because they were able to earn their own money, female merchants like these fruit vendors enjoyed more freedoms than the average medieval woman.

other games. Markets were also cultural centers where poets and musicians took on the roles of merchants as they recited poems or sang songs, hoping for a tip of a few coins or perhaps an orange or piece of bread. Puppet masters, portrait painters, circus performers, and others also tried to capitalize on the free flow of money and goods at the market.

In this atmosphere, medieval markets were great equalizers, some of the only places where county people, city folks, merchants, artists, and wealthy nobles all mingled in close quarters. Some believed, however, that local bazaars were morally objectionable. As Humbert de Romans wrote in 1250, those attending markets, often on Christian holidays, were ignoring their religious obligations. In addition, blasphemous language was used by merchants and their customers when haggling over prices:

> [Markets are for] the daily necessaries of life; they are held weekly and only people from near at hand come. . . . They are held on feast days, and men miss thereby the divine office and the sermon and even disobey the precept of hearing Mass, and attend these meetings against the Church's commands. Sometimes, too, they are held in graveyards and other holy places. Frequently you will hear men swearing there: "By God I will not give you so much for it," or "By God I will not take a smaller price," or "By God it is not worth so much as that." Sometimes again the lord is defrauded of market dues, which is perfidy and disloyalty. . . . Sometimes, too, quarrels happen and violent disputes. . . . Drinking is occasioned. . . . [In] the market-place . . . each man is a devil to himself.[24]

CRIME AND PUNISHMENT

As Romans noted, perfidy, or deliberate violation of trust, was a fact of life in the medieval market. Then, as now, there were always people willing to cheat the public in one manner or another, and merchants were no exception. In most places buyers had to beware of purchasing spoiled meat or shoddy goods. In larger cities, however, merchants were regulated by dozens of laws enforced by an army of officials. In London, the mayor was in charge of controlling the food trade, regulating prices, making sure weights were accurate, and ensuring the quality of goods. The 1378 London Ordinance of Cooks, for example, instructed sellers on the exact price they could charge for the best-quality roasted birds. The ordinance allowed a merchant to charge four and a half pence for a river mallard, two pence for three roasted thrushes, two and a half pence for three pigeons, and

"PUTRID, ROTTEN, STINKING" PIGEONS

In 1365, a London merchant, John Russelle, was put in the pillory for selling inedible pigeons. According to the following fourteenth-century court record, printed in G.G. Coulton's Social Life in Britain: From the Conquest to the Reformation, *Russelle was also forced to smell the rotten meat burning while enduring his punishment:*

John Russelle, on the 15th day of September . . . at Billyngesgate, exposed 37 pigeons for sale, putrid, rotten, stinking, and abominable to the human race, to the scandal, contempt, and disgrace of all the City. . . . And the said John Russelle says the same pigeons are good and proper for sale to mankind, and he offers to prove the same etc. And hereupon, [pie-bakers] John Vygerous, Thomas de Wynchestre . . . [and cooks] John Wenge, Geoffery Colman, John Lowe, Thomas Colman, and Richard de Daventre . . . being sworn to inspect and examine whether pigeons are good and proper or not etc.; say upon their oath, that the said pigeons are not good or wholesome for mankind, but rather to the corruption of man etc. Therefore [John Russelle] is to have judgment of the pillory, and the said pigeons are to be burnt beneath the pillory, and the cause of his punishment is to be there proclaimed.

one pence for ten roasted finches. (To put these prices in perspective, a girl who worked as a servant in a wealthy London merchant's house earned about six pence per week.)

Merchants who charged more than the fixed price were harshly punished for profiteering. Since woodcocks were priced at three pence each and partridges at five pence, one court record states: "The wife of Hildy, the poulterer (chicken farmer), and the wife of John Mede, were committed to prison . . . [because] the wife of Hildy sold four [woodcocks] for 20 pence, and the wife of John Mede refused to take 12 pence for two partridges." [25]

Other cheaters were locked in pillories where they were exposed to public jeers and scorn. In 1366, merchant John Edmond of Essex County, England, was forced to stand in the pillory for one hour because, according to court records, he "exposed for sale . . . one quarter of oats in a sack, and had put a bushel of good oats at the mouth of the sack, all the rest therein being [oats] of worse quality, and of no value, in deceit of the common people." [26]

Such problems often spurred the creation of new laws. In 1379, merchants who sold pies, called pasties, in London were subjected to new regulations that controlled the ingredients in their pies. The law was enacted because merchants "have heretofore baked [into] pasties rabbits, geese, and garbage, not befitting, and sometimes stinking, in deceit of the people; and have also baked beef in pasties, and sold the same for venison."[27]

THE MERCHANT'S FAIR

While markets had their share of dishonest merchants, fairs were considered more respectable because they were mainly patronized by well-established merchants. These annual or biannual fairs lasted up to six weeks and were large open-air bazaars where merchants could buy and sell among themselves.

Fairs were held at crossroads of important trade routes. The Geneva fair was located on the Rhone River, the Fair of St. Denis on the Seine below Paris, and the Frankfurt fair on the Main River. The most famous fair was held in the Champagne region where the major east-west trade road route crossed the Seine River south of Paris.

The Champagne district had nine fairs, established in the twelfth century by local counts who guaranteed the merchants' security on the road in exchange for admittance fees paid by the businessmen. These fairs were spread throughout the year. The major ones, such as the January–February fair at Lagny, lasted six weeks. In March and April, during Lent, another festival took place at Bar-sur-Aube. The town of Troyes hosted the "Hot Fair" in July and August and the "Cold Fair" in November–December. Other fairs held in between these fairs were smaller and shorter in duration. These fairs were extremely important for merchants who specialized in specific products. For example, cloth merchants from sixty "cloth towns" in northwest Europe sold their wares exclusively at Champagne fairs.

While the fairs were organized primarily for business purposes, they also provided entertainment, as Joseph and Frances Gies note in *Merchants and Moneymen:* "[A] six-week Fair was a noisy, lively, many-languaged Babel, with gawking peasants and knights as audience for the show, which included real show people like acrobats, jugglers, and sleight-of-hand artists, as well as cooks, taverners [barkeepers], and prostitutes."[28]

WORKING THE FAIR

To work the fairs, merchants who lived in distant regions formed companies so that they could travel together, often in armed groups to protect themselves from bandits. Company officers included a captain, in charge of the entire business; consuls to represent company members to fair officials; and workers called harbingers who arrived up to eight days early to unpack the wares and set up stalls.

The fairs at Champagne were organized in four main phases. The first was a week of entry when merchants registered with the Keeper of the Fair and competed for the best booth locations, stables, storage, and lodgings. The other three phases are explained by the Gieses:

[The second phase was] a ten-day Cloth Market during which the Italians examined, priced, and bargained over the varieties of wool cloth displayed by the men of Ghent, Ypres, Bruges, Arras, and the other cloth cities; third came a month-long "avoir de poids," [a market where goods are sold by weight] during which

This woodcut shows a medieval merchant fair in Germany. Open for business for up to six weeks, these fairs typically attracted well-established merchants.

ॐ THE FAIR OF ST. DENIS ॐ

One of the earliest records of a medieval fair comes from June 30, 629, announcing the Fair of St. Denis, or Dionysius, in Paris. The proclamation, printed in The Records of Medieval Europe, *shows that even in this early era, merchants came from many points in Europe to sell their wares—and the charging of all manner of tolls was a constant problem:*

Dagobert, king of the Franks, to the illustrious . . . counts and all our agents, vicars, hundredmen [law enforcement officers], and other ministers of our republic. . . . [We] have set up a market in honor of our lord and glorious patron Dionysius . . . consisting of all the tradesmen in our kingdom and those who come from across the sea. . . . We order, moreover, that the same market be extended throughout four weeks, so that traders from Lombardy or Spain or Provence or from other regions are able to come to it. . . . Finally, we command and expressly order you, and all of your agents or apprentices or successors present and to come, that there be no impediment of any kind, to this, Saint Dionysius', market . . . from tolls or waterway-taxes, bridge-tolls, river-tolls . . . navigational tolls, camp-tolls . . . [or] wine tolls . . . levied anywhere or by anyone, except those that can be exacted on the merchandise of the fair on our behalf or for the public [good].

A fourteenth-century painting depicts the Fair of St. Denis in Paris, one of the earliest recorded medieval merchant fairs.

nontextile commodities, but above all spices, were sold, as Italians and Flemings [Belgians] exchanged roles of salesmen and customers. The final week was reserved for the *pagamentum* or settling of accounts, not only to the jingle of silver [coins], but to the scratch of quills and styluses, for credit transactions grew steadily in volume, helping shape a significant element of the commercial future.[29]

The Champagne fairs dominated the trade circuit, but plenty of other fairs were well established in medieval Europe. The Flanders fair in present-day Belgium, for example, was dedicated to cloth merchants, and dried and pickled fish was sold by the barrel at the herring fair in Skane, Sweden. Few fairs were as prestigious or comfortable for merchants as those in Champagne, however. For example, the fair in Westminster was often ruined by the typically rainy English weather, as Matthew of Paris wrote in 1288:

[All] the merchants, in exposing their goods for sale there, were exposed to great inconveniences, as they had no shelter except canvas tents; for owing to the changeable gusts of wind assailing them, as is usual at that time of the year, they were cold and wet, and also suffered from hunger and thirst; their feet were soiled by the mud, and their goods rotted by the showers of rain.[30]

Such conditions prompted some traders to devise means to profit from fairs without ever leaving the comfort of their homes. For example, the merchant Symon di Gualterio used credit, loans, and contracts to work this way. With letters of credit, Gualterio was able to purchase thirty bolts of English cloth through trusted agents at a Champagne fair in March 1253. The money was repaid after the goods were sold, and the profits were used to buy spices, including twelve bales of ginger, that were retailed through Italian agents at the fair in Provins, France, in May. These profits, in turn, were invested in cloth that was shipped to Genoa. In *Power and Profit: The Merchant in Medieval Europe,* Peter Spufford explains how merchants financed such complicated transactions:

It became possible for Italian merchants to extend credit to their customers from one fair to the next. It also became possible for Italian merchants with funds to spare, after they had sold their goods, to make loans to others from one fair to the next, and in turn to be repaid not at a future fair but in Italy. Merchants in Italy could also arrange for money to be sent to Champagne.

Even private individuals used these nascent banking facilities for moving money about. [31]

THE MEDIEVAL BOOM

This free flow of money enriched people in all segments of medieval society. Nobles were growing increasingly wealthier from the rents they charged to fair organizers. Nobles were, of course, customers too, flocking to the fairs to spend money, patronizing craftspeople, tailors, goldsmiths, grocers, and retailers. The nobility put their gold and silver into the hands of merchants, who in turn spent it on hotels, restaurants, entertainment, and, of course, more merchandise. This circle of wealth attracted support workers from miles around and spurred the growth of towns. For example, the Provins fairs were first held in the late eleventh century on a small piece of land outside the castle of a local count. As the fair grew in popularity, it was moved to a large space at a local churchyard nearby. During the twelfth century, an entire town grew up around the fair site as enterprising peasants opened up inns, taverns, stables, and other businesses that catered to the merchants.

Merchants also spurred the development of monetary standards. For example, when the Provins mint opened in the tenth century, the coins it minted were only used locally. By the 1170s, because of merchant trade, Provins coins were the main currency throughout eastern France and central Italy.

Similar standardization developed for weights and measures. Originally, troy weight, the method of measuring precious metals and gemstones, was only used in Troyes, France. As the trade fairs in Troyes gained popularity, troy weight became the standard for measuring goods from Paris to London, adopted by jewelers even into the modern era.

THE END OF THE FAIRS

During the twelfth and thirteenth centuries, few merchants could imagine a world without Champagne trade fairs. By the fourteenth century, however, several factors contributed to their decline. A war instituted in 1297 by French king Philip IV in the regions north of Champagne brought trade between Bruges and Paris to a halt even as Philip raised taxes on merchants to pay for the war. Even more devastating was the development of improved ships and navigational equipment that allowed merchants to sail directly from Italy to the cloth cities of northern Europe without having to pass through Champagne. The final blow to the Champagne fair was its own success. After so many merchants had established contacts with one another at the fair, they began to conduct business together directly.

A merchant fair is shown in this medieval drawing. By the fourteenth century, large fairs became obsolete, as merchants began to conduct business with each other directly.

This negated the need to travel to Champagne to make contacts.

Even as towns in the Champagne region adjusted to this harsh reality, weekly markets continued to thrive and become daily markets in many places. The merchants followed the money, sometimes profiting and sometimes losing, as their goods improved their customers' lives.

CHAPTER 3

MERCHANT GUILDS

As trade and commerce became widely established in the second half of the Middle Ages, the number of merchants buying and selling trade goods expanded rapidly. Many European merchants traveled in groups for safety, lived with one another at fairs, and routinely conducted business together. They had mutual interests: dealing with government officials concerning taxes and tariffs, market regulations, trade routes, and even matters of war and peace. Considering these circumstances, it was natural that by the late eleventh century merchants would form representative organizations, called guilds. Sometimes spelled *gild,* these organizations are defined by Georges Renard in *Guilds in the Middle Ages:* "The guild was a voluntary association of men [and sometimes women] carrying on the same trade or allied trades and pledging themselves by oath to defend their common interests." [32]

Merchant guilds were first established in individual towns so members could obtain—and maintain—the exclusive right to carry on trade in a certain area. Guilds were granted their special status, privileges, and authority in charters issued directly by kings, such as the directive of King John, who issued a guild charter to merchants of Ipswich, England, in 1200: "We grant a Gild Merchant with a [meeting house] and other customs . . . so that no one who is not of the Gild may merchandise in the said town." [33]

MAINTAINING MONOPOLIES

Merchant guilds existed in Holland, France, Italy, England, and elsewhere and took many forms. All had several objectives in common, however. The primary purpose of the guilds was to maintain a monopoly over all buying and selling in a particular market, or concerning specific products. This is demonstrated in a record of a meeting in Venice in 1283, called to establish a guild, known as a *societas,* Latin for "fellowship": "[Our] merchants present [here] shall form a *societas* for [the purchase] of cotton, buckram [stiff cotton fabric], and pepper . . . and nobody may purchase [the aforesaid wares] except those [representatives of the *societas*] appointed for that purpose."[34]

Foreigners or local merchants who were not members of a guild were forced to pay tolls, taxes, and tariffs if they wanted to import goods to a town or participate in a local market. This forced the outsiders to charge higher prices, giving guild merchants a competitive advantage.

Guilds often influenced governments to maintain monopolies on a large scale. For example, at the behest of twelfth-century guilds, rulers of the powerful Byzantine Empire, centered in Constantinople, banned Western ships

A medieval wood panel shows different merchant guilds. Guilds helped merchants maintain monopolies on their respective trades.

from the Black Sea. This preserved the entire eastern European trade region for Byzantine merchant traders. As political power changed hands in the 1200s, Venetian and Genoese guilds each exerted their influence by monopolizing trade on the Black Sea. In the early 1300s, Georgios Pachymeres wrote about the situation enjoyed by the Genoese guilds on the Black Sea around 1275: "[Once] the Genoese became masters of the Black Sea by grant of the emperor and with all liberty and franchise, they braved that [sea] and . . . not only barred the Romans from the lanes and the wares of the sea but also eclipsed the Venetians in wealth and material [goods]."[35]

STRICT REGULATIONS

While maintaining trade monopolies, guilds prevented monopolies within their own ranks. That is, an enterprising guild member who worked harder or more efficiently, or who tried to gain great wealth at the expense of others, was pressured by a number of guild restraints. Rempel explains how guilds maintained equality among members:

◌ RULES OF THE GUILD ◌

Merchant guilds were ruled by charters that spelled out rules and regulations for the members. Excerpts from the following fourteenth-century Southampton charter, published on the Medieval Source-book Web site, seem primarily concerned with alcoholic beverages for its officers:

In the first place, there shall be elected from the gild merchant, and established, an alderman, a steward, a chaplain . . . and an usher. . . . And the gild shall meet twice a year. . . .

And when the gild shall sit, the alderman is to have, each night, so long as the gild sits, two gallons of wine and two candles, and the steward the same; and . . . the chaplain . . . one gallon of wine and one candle, and the usher one gallon of wine. . . .

And when the gild sits, and any gildsman is outside of the city so that he does not know when it will happen, he shall have a gallon of wine, if his servants come to get it. And if a gildsman is ill and is in the city, wine shall be sent to him, two loaves of bread and a gallon of wine and a dish from the kitchen; and two approved men of the gild shall go to visit him and look after his condition. . . .

And no one shall buy honey, fat, salt herrings, or any kind of oil, or millstones, or fresh hides, or any kind of fresh skins, unless he is a gildsman . . . and whoever shall do this and be convicted, shall forfeit all to the king.

The attempts of the guilds to maintain equality among their members . . . took [the] form of regulations concerning technical processes, hours of labor, wages, number of workmen to be employed, prices and trade practices of all sorts. Every effort was made to nip the capitalist spirit in the bud. One regulation common in the merchant guilds guaranteed to every member the right to participate in any purchase made by any other guildsmen; that is, it was considered unfair for any one member to derive advantage from a particular bargain.[36]

Punishment for disobeying such regulations could be severe in some cases. Lopez and Raymond note that in tenth-century Constantinople members of the raw-silk dealers' guild who violated standard practices were to be "beaten and shaved and expelled from the guild."[37]

In this manner, guilds stifled not only competition but also progress. If a merchant discovered a new, more efficient way to manufacture the goods he sold, he was punished unless he shared it with other guild members. If a merchant paid workers with greater skills or higher wages, he was fined or punished. Advertising was forbidden, and no merchant could try to lure another's workers or customers to his shop. And all members had to charge

Guild membership assured merchants like this fish dealer that their goods would fetch fair market value.

the same price for specific goods. When a herring merchant in Yaxley, England, sold his fish for a cheaper price than others, guild members "assaulted him, beat him and ill-treated him and left him there for dead, so that he despaired of his life."[38]

While guild members had the power to inflict such pain on their fellow guildsmen, they needed to treat their customers fairly. If they did not, the king might revoke their charter, thus putting them all out of business. For this reason, guilds ensured that merchants were honest and that their goods were of reasonable quality and fairly priced. To do so, guilds employed a host of enforcers to impose rules on merchants. English guilds, which were active in about 150 towns, used wardens to oversee manufacturing processes. "Levelookers" inspected the quality of provisions brought to market, while gatewaiters stood at city gates in order to stop foreign merchants from entering. Tasters sampled food to ensure that it was not spoiled.

"GOOD REPUTATION, PURE LIFE"

To become a member of a guild, a merchant paid an initiation fee and membership dues. The rate was adjusted so that poorer merchants paid less than the wealthy. Membership in many guilds was restricted to relatives of other members. Family connections were essential, one reason why marriages were arranged for their contractual value. Initiates were also expected to provide references who guaranteed the newcomer's moral conduct and who would pledge to fulfill his obligations to the guild and pay his dues if he faltered. In Florence, according to Renard, "a man had to be respected for his piety, his good reputation, his pure life, and proven honesty; he must be faithful and devoted to the Holy Roman Church, sound in mind and body, and born in lawful wedlock. . . . Punishments were inflicted on blasphemers, players of games of chance, and even usurers [money lenders]."[39] Upon acceptance into a guild, the guild member took

an oath of faithfulness to the guild, swore to observe its laws, and promised not to aid any merchant, such as a foreigner, who was not in the guild. Those who did aid non–guild members or who violated other guild rules were expelled from the guild, shunned by members, and often forced out of business. An unidentified member of a guild in Andover, England, was punished for an unnamed offense when the guild ordered "that no one receive him, nor buy and sell with him, nor give him fire or water, nor hold communication with him, under penalty of loss of [membership]."[40]

The most important guild business was entrusted to officers who acted as a general assembly, making and sanctioning rules and acting as judges in disputes. Some guilds had many such officers. In Italy, guilds elected four consuls, a cashier, a proctor or supervisor, a syndic—a business agent—and several notaries. In addition, there were many junior officers, such as assistant consuls, and so on.

These officers were elected by various means. In Florence, they were appointed by the wealthiest members of the guild to act in their interests. In Toulouse, France, the municipal magistrates appointed guild officers. Among members of the butchers guild in Arra, Italy, officers were chosen by chance. Each member was represented by a ball of wax that was put into an urn. Only one ball, however,

❧ THE GUILDHALL ❧

Merchant guilds were prosperous organizations that used membership dues to build great halls where members could conduct business, hold meetings, and have parties. Oftentimes guildhalls were the finest buildings for miles around. The Merchant Adventurers' Hall in York, England, for example, was one of the largest buildings in Britain when it was completed in 1360.

Each merchant guild had its own coat of arms that hung in the hall. Many had symbols of the merchant trade, such as boats, mercantile goods, grain, or sheep. Halls were hung with many banners decorated in a similar manner. Banners displayed patron saints, tools of the merchant trade, and royal symbols affiliated with the guild.

Great halls of guilds were decorated with some of the finest available tables, chairs, tapestries, and paintings. Small offices contained large locked chests filled with important documents, coins, and other valuables belonging to the guild. Archives, written on rolls of parchment paper, covered topics including bank accounts, title deeds, guild rules, and royal charters.

had the words "Jesus-Marie" inscribed on it. Every member pulled a ball of wax out of the urn, and the man who chose the inscribed ball was appointed head of the guild for several years.

WOMEN IN THE GUILDS

Although members of guilds were generally referred to as guildsmen, some guilds included women. Women had the same rights and obligations as men but sometimes had to meet additional conditions before being allowed to join a guild. For example, a woman might have to call witnesses to prove that she was chaste—that is, morally pure and sexually restrained.

Guild women were either merchants with their own businesses or daughters of guildsmen who worked for their fathers. Despite their status as independent traders, guild women were expected to defer to men. In one instance a town council forced a guild woman to apologize to a male customer because she had repeatedly pressed him to make good on his unpaid bills. In other cases guilds gave men the authority to collect debts owed to women merchants on their behalf because the women were not allowed by custom to approach men to request their money.

Although they were restricted, women were well represented in guilds despite the conservative attitudes of the time. For example, in Genoa in 1205, 21 percent of people signing trade contracts were guild women.

MEETING, EATING, AND DRINKING

The women and men of the guilds met in their guildhalls annually, biannually, or quarterly. The meeting halls were often the finest buildings in town, as a twelfth-century description of a guildhall in Yarmouth, England, makes clear: "The hall itself being at that time richly hanged and adorned with cloth of [finest] Tapestry, and other costly furniture; not sparing any dainty fare which might be had for money." [41]

During meetings, new members were confirmed, wayward members were punished, and new regulations were discussed, debated, and voted on by members. After business was taken care of, members spent the rest of

A medieval painting shows merchants meeting in their guildhall. After discussing business, guild members typically spent the rest of their meetings feasting and carousing.

the meeting drinking, eating, and pursuing other amusements. Massive quantities of beer and wine, staple beverages of the era, were served to guild officers, called aldermen and stewards, who were allotted two gallons of wine per meeting. Lower-ranked members received only one gallon each. Ancient records also tell of members feasting on roast beef, geese, and spice cake.

A favorite entertainment was bullbaiting. For this popular amusement, new members were required to provide a bull to the guild. This animal was then tethered to a stake while vicious bulldogs attacked it. Sometimes the maddened bull broke free and charged at the audience, increasing the hilarity for some.

PROVIDING FOR MEMBERS

Guilds provided more than feasts and bullbaiting spectacles for their members. Outreach programs for children of members encouraged them to learn to read, write, and do arithmetic—useful skills for keeping business records. Guilds also took care of their members who fell on hard times, providing assistance in times of sickness and poverty. Some guilds even owned and operated their own hospitals.

A guild played a very important role when a member died, as the Southampton charter reveals:

And when a gildsman dies, all those who are of the gild and are

in the city shall attend the service of the dead, and the gildsmen shall bear the body and bring it to the place of burial. And whoever will not do this shall pay . . . two pence, to be given to the poor. And those of the [guild shall] . . . find a man to watch over the body the night that the dead shall lie in his house. And so long as the service of the dead shall last, that is to say the vigil and the mass, there ought to burn four candles of the gild, each candle of two pounds weight or more, until the body is buried. And these four candles shall remain in the keeping of the steward of the gild. [42]

During such events, guild merchants would shutter their shops so that everyone could attend the funeral.

Guilds were also charitable organizations that donated to the sick and needy. In fourteenth-century Southampton, guild members provided staple beverages for the poverty stricken and the disabled living in various convalescent homes:

And when the gild shall sit, the lepers of La Madeleine shall have of the alms of the gild, two sesters (approximately eight gallons) of ale, and the sick of God's House and of St. Julian shall have two sesters of ale. And the Friars Minors shall have two sesters of ale and

one sester of wine. And four sesters of ale shall be given to the poor
wherever the gild shall meet.[43]

Guilds also contributed money to
charities. Each guild kept a financial
aid fund, known as a "chest," sup-
plied by membership dues, fines, and
voluntary donations from guild members. On occasion, the chest even provided a dowry for poor girls whose fathers were in the fraternity.

Sometimes merchants donated their
products to charity. For example, in
Alsace, on the border of France and
Germany, bylaws of the bakers guild
stated that the sick in hospitals were
to be provided daily with a good loaf
of bread, along with confession, com-
munion, and a clean bed.

"UNCONTESTED SUPREMACY"

While guilds were notable for their
charitable contributions, they were
mainly concerned with enriching their
members. And at a time when average
people had little power to oppose the
nobility, the guild system proved to be
quite successful in creating a special
place in medieval society for merchants. The success, however, changed
the guilds from semidemocratic institutions working on behalf of average
merchants to organizations representing the interests of the richest,
most influential members of society
outside the nobility. As Renard writes,

*This illustration depicts members of a
shipbuilders' guild at work. Guild members
were prominent members of medieval society.*

guilds were "the first to succeed in
making their power felt, and represented, first by right of priority, and
later by right of wealth, all that existed in the way of business . . . and they
long retained an uncontested su-
premacy."[44]

Guilds' wealth, and monopolistic
control of all trade goods, allowed
guild members to employ a growing

number of nonagricultural workers in towns and cities. Guild staffs included cashiers, bookkeepers, porters, brokers, agents, carriers, and messengers whose performance was strictly monitored. Those who disobeyed—or were caught stealing—were fined, imprisoned, tortured, and even excommunicated from the church. Renard explains how guild members in Florence used this system to their advantage:

> At some periods of its existence this guild had a membership of 20,000 to 30,000, but it was like a pyramid, with a very large base, numerous tiers, and a very small apex. At the summit were the masters, who were recruited entirely from among the rich families and formed a solid alliance for the defense of their own interests. Forced to guard against the perils which threatened their business on every hand—the difficulty of transport, a foreign country closed to them by war or by a tariff, the jealousy of rival towns—they tried to recoup themselves by employing cheap labour, and, remembering the maxim "divide and rule," they ranked the workmen they employed in different degrees of dependence and poverty.

> Some classes of workers . . . were kept under strict rules and under the vow to obey officers nominated by the masters alone. Thus . . .

[they] were not allowed to work on their own account, and were subjected to heavy fines if the goods entrusted to them suffered the slightest damage; the rate of wages was fixed, but not the date of payment, which was invariably delayed. [45]

LIFE IN THE KONTOR

The more powerful the guild, the stricter the rules governing its members. Between the twelfth and sixteenth centuries, trade in northern Europe was rigorously controlled by the Hanseatic League, which was an organization of merchants from over one hundred towns in Germany and northern Europe. Known as Hansa, or Hanse, a German word for "guild," this powerful organization had dozens of rules to control merchant members.

Hansa maintained special offices, known as Kontors, in London, Bruges, and about two dozen other cities where members of the guilds lived while on trading missions. The rules at the Kontors made the guild members virtual prisoners while traveling. Paul Schulz explains in the article "The Hanseatic League (Hansa)":

> The austerity of the leagues' representatives in foreign posts was shown in the rules imposed upon them. They could not leave the post at night. Guards, watch dogs and iron doors enforced this rule.

They could associate with the people of the country for business purposes, but were not allowed to fraternize or marry while abroad. Business dealings were to be rigidly honest so as to avoid bringing the ire of the local people upon all of the representatives. However advantages more than made up for these restrictions. Merchants were exempt from tolls and taxes paid by others and, on occasion, had a monopoly of a certain trade. [46]

The Hanseatic League's depot in London is shown in this medieval drawing. As one of the most powerful guilds, the Hanseatic League had very strict rules of membership.

THE POWERFUL GERMAN HANSA

In the 1100s, maritime merchants in Germany formed the Hanseatic League to protect their mutual interests. As Paul Schulz writes in "The Hanseatic League (Hansa)" Web article, its power far outstripped that of any king or church for several centuries:

The Hansa then grew out of a loose confederation of medieval northern German towns where they had the need for mutual protection for their convoys and caravans against piracy and marauding land barons. . . .

The main weapons of the Hansa were boycott and commercial monopoly. The merchants of a town that refused to join would often be unable to sell their products in a profitable market. . . .

The Hansa had conducted trade wars against England, Norway and Flanders, but special alliances had to be made among individual cities where there were military wars. . . .

The league controlled the fur trade with Russia, the fish trade with Norway and Sweden and the wool trade with Flanders. Its other accomplishments were: checking piracy on the Baltic and North Seas, establishing maritime and commercial laws, preparing charts and navigational aids, carrying comforts and conveniences into remote lands and the exchanging of ideas throughout Northern Europe.

Those who were willing to follow the rules and wanted to join Hansa were subject to bizarre hazing rituals. In Bergen, Norway, initiates marched down the street carrying buckets that they filled with scraps of garbage, old horsehair, and horse manure they found along the road. Senior members marched along with them in masks and costumes. After this parade, a candidate was suspended high within a wide chimney. Below him the filth from the bucket was set aflame in the hearth. As E. Gee Nash writes in *The Hansa: Its History and Romance:* "Nauseated, stifled and half dead from the appalling stench, the victim was lowered from time to time and put through severe questioning. Then, when almost at the end of his endurance, he was let down, carried out into the central courtyard of the Kontor and drenched with six [barrels] of water."[47]

The trial by smoke was avoided by those who were initiated around Pentecost (the seventh Sunday after Easter). Instead, these guild members were forced to undergo initiation by water. Placed naked in a boat and rowed out to sea, they were repeatedly plunged into the water and beaten when they came up for air. Since the Hansa barred women from membership, this initiation was originally done to test the sex of the candidates, as a woman once tried to pass herself off as a man to get into the guild.

The strange initiation rites of the Hansa were not typical of guilds in England and Italy. They do show, however, the pains merchants would endure in order to join such a prestigious organization. Until their decline during the Industrial Revolution in the eighteenth century, guilds provided members with social, political, and monetary power unavailable to other citizens of medieval towns.

CHAPTER 4

EDUCATING AND TRAINING THE MERCHANT CLASS

During the Middle Ages, virtually all peasants were illiterate. Reading was considered an elite skill practiced only by aristocrats and clergymen. Those who wanted to learn to read had to hire tutors, attend expensive monastery schools, or join religious orders. Since most schools were run by churches, students were mainly taught to read religious rites and Bible stories. Reading was usually in Latin and much less often in what were referred to as the "vulgar" languages of English, French, or German.

Once a person could read, in this age before printing presses and bookstores, he or she had to purchase costly manuscripts that were individually copied out by hand on parchment paper made from goat, calf, or even squirrel skin. In the few universities that existed, these books, illustrated with beautiful handmade paintings, were chained to tables to prevent theft. As commercial activities grew and developed after the eleventh century, however, merchants inspired a revolution in education.

A DEMAND FOR SCHOOLS

In the early years of mercantilism, a merchant simply needed to know the

An image from a medieval manuscript shows a merchant using a payment ledger.

local language and be able to keep track of the money and merchandise in his possession. As trade grew and became international, merchants found that they at least needed to be able to read, write, and understand arithmetic. To be successful, a merchant also had to be well versed in foreign languages and customs, contracts, exchange rates, credit practices, and other complex business standards. While most mer-

chants learned on the job, some hired teachers, local clergymen, or local professionals such as lawyers to teach them the basics. In college towns such as Oxford, Paris, and Bologna, merchants sometimes traded room and board for lessons from college students. As Favier writes:

[A] cobbler [named] Azemar Couronne of Toulouse did not think

As trade expanded to more distant ports, merchants like these were forced to learn different languages and to study the customs of foreign cultures.

twice about engaging a student from Albi for a whole year to teach both his son and himself. . . . The young man had to pay six francs for his meals; it would appear that the opportunity of free lodging in a university town was not to be sneered at. In this case, the employer even promised to supply free candles so that [the student] could continue his own studies in the evening.[48]

As educated merchants became more successful, they created a demand for schools that specialized in business-related curricula. Some schools were set up by town governments, but most were founded by scholars who wanted to profit by teaching the children of well-to-do merchants. By the beginning of the fourteenth century, nearly every substantial town and city in Europe had at least one school specializing in mercantilism. Venice alone had 150 such private institutions, which paid their teachers better than any other in Europe.

In Venice and elsewhere in Italy, schools that trained merchants were called abacus schools because students learned, among other computational skills, to use a version of the abacus, an ancient counting device. In the town of Villani, six abacus schools catered to the needs of twelve hundred children. While other schools may have taught a broader-based curriculum, abacus schools were often limit-ed to teaching subjects relating to business. In Genoa, for example, teachers' contracts from 1307 stipulate that pupils will only learn as much Latin "as is suitable to merchants."[49]

Those who wanted to continue their education could attend some of the many universities that were established in cities across Europe beginning in the twelfth century. These included the University of Bologna, the University of Paris, and Oxford and Cambridge universities in England. By the thirteenth century, dozens of other universities were founded in places such as Cologne, Pisa, Florence, Avignon, and elsewhere.

THE SCIENCE OF MATHEMATICS

A business education involved study in a host of subjects. After basic literacy, the most important skills were mathematical, beginning with addition, subtraction, division, multiplication, and computations involving fractions. Competence in geometry and astronomy was helpful for those wishing to sail across the seas using the stars for navigation.

Knowledge of mathematics had been nearly nonexistent in Europe until around the eleventh century. This began to change when Italian merchants began doing business with Arabs whose contributions to mathematics in the Middle Ages included the use of fractions, the concept of

❧ A REVOLUTION IN ARITHMETIC ❧

In the tenth century, few were familiar with the concepts of simple arithmetic. The commercial revolution spurred by merchants changed that, as Stephen E. Sachs writes in the Web article "The 'Countinghouse Theory' and the Medieval Revival of Arithmetic":

The period from the eleventh century to the thirteenth was one of unprecedented mathematical advance . . . , [because of] commerce. Buying or selling goods for money relies on familiarity with numbers, and sharing goods or collecting revenues requires division and multiplication; above all, money . . . provides a means of exact measure for an abstract quality such as value. . . .

It may be difficult to imagine that any society would long be unfamiliar with the basic concepts of arithmetic; yet . . .

[the] West of the Early Middle Ages . . . certainly seems to be an age in which popular numeracy—the ability to use numbers, as literacy is the capacity to make use of written expression—was significantly curtailed. . . .

The first signs of change came in the late tenth century, when . . . new mathematical instruments and techniques began to emerge. . . . Yet what fueled this evolution? . . . [Arithmetic] was revived by the needs of commerce—this is the countinghouse theory of mathematical origins. [It can be traced] directly to interaction with the financial and commercial interests of the Arab world; Italian merchants adopted the arithmetic in the twelfth century and introduced it to their native lands, where it was taught in the schools.

zero, and the method of writing numerical digits from left to right. These merchants were also exposed to mathematical concepts developed in India, including the decimal system, negative numbers, compound interest, and geometry.

Before long, schools were teaching mathematics to students beginning at age eleven. Italy, at the heart of merchant culture, was known as one of the best places in the world to study mathematics, and some cities even hosted popular public lectures on the subject of algebra. In Venice, Florence, and Genoa, merchants kept their children in school until age fifteen— at least four years longer than those who lived in France and Germany. Italian children were taught complex mathematical algorithms, the application of predetermined rules to problem solving. They were also taught bookkeeping and accounting skills and the concept of ratios, which was indispensable for merchants who needed to quickly convert dozens of different currencies. In the early thirteenth century, Fibonacci, known as the greatest European mathematician of the Middle Ages, recalled how he was directed to study math:

When my father, who had been appointed . . . as public notary in the customs . . . for the Pisan merchants . . . summoned me to him while I was still a child, and having an eye to usefulness and future convenience, desired me to stay there and receive instruction in the school of accounting. There, when I had been introduced to the art of [mathematics] through remarkable teaching, knowledge of the art very soon pleased me above all else and I came to understand it . . . in all its various forms. [50]

Fibonacci went on to write a popular book, *Liber abaci,* in 1202, which contains a large collection of arithmetical problems aimed at merchants. They related to the price of goods, how profits may be calculated on transactions, and how various currencies in use in Mediterranean countries could be converted. This book, each edition meticulously copied by hand, was used as a text for teaching throughout Italy.

In addition to math, students learned about geography and economics as it applied to business. Studies included the location of trading towns and the routes available to merchants. Each town was identified by what merchandise was bought and sold there, along with the laws and tariffs that governed trade. While lawyers actually wrote and executed contracts, students were instructed in basic terminology so that they would not be cheated.

Students and businessmen also took language courses so they could speak at least rudimentary Italian, English, French, German, or Flemish. As in other aspects of commerce, however,

Because so much of their business involved weights, measures, and numbers, medieval merchants needed a basic understanding of mathematics.

Italians had the linguistic advantage. Much like English today, during the medieval period Italian was the international language of business and trading. Italians lived in nearly every major European city, and those who wanted to do business with them were expected to speak Italian whether they were natives of Paris, London, Munich, or Moscow.

THE STUDENT LIFE

While young men dreamed of making fortunes in exotic cities, students often lived in near poverty while attending school away from home. Many lodged in boardinghouses run by elderly women who set up three or four beds in a single room where students slept. Students had to provide their own blankets, pillows, and sheets, which were very expensive at the time. In 1168, Alexander Neckam described the bedding in his student room: "A quilted pad of striped cloth . . . [covers this bed] on which a cushion for the head can be placed. The sheets of muslin, ordinary cotton, or at least pure linen, should be laid. Next a coverlet of green cloth or of coarse wool, of which the fur lining is badger, cat, beaver, or sable."[51]

The walls of Neckam's room were hung with thick cloth curtains to keep out flies and spiders, to stop cold drafts, and to give the primitive stone walls a better appearance. In many boardinghouses, the beds were folded into corners during the day, and the same room was used as a dining hall and lounge. Large wooden chests were placed along the walls so students could store their clothing, books, and other meager possessions. Benches, rickety chairs, and small rugs on the floor provided places for students to sit and study by candlelight. If the room lacked a warming fireplace, a large metal plate was provided in which coal could be burned.

Students paid for their own meals; twice a day, the hostess cooked whatever food the lodgers could afford, while a man, usually her husband, served beverages. In 1184, author Johannes de Hauvilla described one such scene, writing that students "dwell in a poor house with an old woman who cooks only vegetables. . . . A dirty fellow waits on the table and just such a person buys wine in the city."[52] John of Garland described the food situation in his student boardinghouse:

I eat sparingly in my little room, not high up in a castle. I have no silver money, nor do the Fates give me estates. Beets, beans, and peas are here looked upon as fine dishes and we joke about the meat, which is not in our menu for a very good reason [as it is rotten]. The size of the wine skin on the table depends on the purse, which is never large.[53]

An apprentice (right) works in a merchant's shop in this medieval woodcut. In addition to mastering a trade, the apprentice also obtained an education in math and language.

THE MERCHANT APPRENTICE

While living the life of a frugal student, students often honed their knowledge of business on the job. Children as young as ten, when not in school, served as apprentices in offices where they learned how to apply mathemat- ics, language, and geography to real- life situations. This included making deals, keeping books, changing mon- ey, and buying and selling merchan- dise.

Older students were expected to help organize and update account- ing books, usually for their fathers or other family members. Some apprentices worked with accountants using abaci, complex counting tables that looked something like chess boards. Roman numerals were inscribed in each square, and colored pebbles were used to mark specific numbers relevant to the business at hand. In *The Merchant of Prato,* Iris Origo describes the scene of apprentices working with an accountant in fourteenth-century Italy:

> In a secluded corner [of the merchant's shop], in front of a cupboard containing his account-books, sat the scrivener or accountant—often with a mirror on the wall to reflect the scanty light on to his ledger—and beside him on a table stood a large square counting-board, with some bowls or little sacks containing counters [pebbles] of various colours. This board was the medieval merchant's [abacus], and was used for keeping his accounts, as smaller similar boards were used for teaching arithmetic in schools. The board was divided into seven columns: the counters representing *denari* [monetary units] . . . were placed in the first column on the right, the *soldi* in the second, and the *lire* . . . in the third, multiples of *lire* extending up to the seventh column, that of the tens of thousands. The

merchant or accountant sat at the table, while a boy handed him the counters he required, and other apprentices crowded round to watch him and [practice accounting].[54]

Apprenticeship also involved travel, and many who worked for family businesses accompanied their fathers, grandfathers, uncles, and brothers on trade missions. Such trips could be quite extensive. Apprentice Buonaccorso Pitti left Florence in 1372 at the age of eighteen. During the next fourteen years, he visited London two times, Paris fifteen times, Bruges five times, and cities such as Heidelberg, Munich, and Zagreb at least once. It was not until 1386, at the age of thirty-two, that he was able to take over the family business. The most famous Italian adventurer, Marco Polo, began his career at age seventeen as an apprentice merchant, traveling with his father and uncle to Mongolia, Constantinople, and elsewhere before making his renowned journey to China and the fabled court of Mongol ruler Kublai Khan.

LEARNING FROM MERCHANT MANUALS

Wherever merchants traveled, they relied on merchant manuals. These were almanacs filled with information that helped them conduct business at home and in foreign lands, as John E.

Dotson explains in *Merchant Culture in the Fourteenth Century: The Zibaldone da Canal:*

Much of a typical merchant's manual was taken up with conversions of weights, measures, and moneys, of which there were a bewildering variety in medieval Europe. They also included information on local conditions, such as general business conditions, taxes to be paid, goods to be found in the markets, and so forth. A merchant's manual also often informed its reader how he might recognize quality in the merchandise he might be about to buy and, occasionally, of common frauds worked to conceal poor quality goods.[55]

⚜ MARCO POLO'S MERCHANT TRAINING ⚜

The most famous medieval European traveler, Marco Polo, began his adventures in 1271 as a seventeen-year-old merchant-in-training. His father and uncle, Nicolo and Maffeo Polo, were successful Venetian jewel merchants who brought the young Marco Polo with them on their second overland trade expedition to the fabled court of the Mongol ruler of China, Kublai Khan. It is likely that in 1271 Polo already spoke French and Italian and had a basic grasp of accounting skills. He would also acquire fluency in Mongolian, Chinese, Persian, and Uighur during his twenty-four-year absence from Venice. Polo's practical training is clear in his observations about goods, taxation, profits, and business opportunities such as these in his influential travelogue, The Book of Marco Polo:

About Kublai Khan's capital city, Peking: "To the city also are brought articles of greater cost and rarity, and in greater abundance of all kinds, than to any other city in the world. . . . As a sample, I tell you, no day in the year passes that there do not enter the city 1,000 carts of silk alone, from which are made quantities of cloth of silk and gold."

About the taxation of goods in the trade center of Hangchow: "In this city and its dependencies they make great quantities of sugar . . . and the sugar alone again produces an enormous revenue. All spices pay three and a third percent on the value; and all merchandise likewise pays three and a third percent. (But sea-borne goods from India and other distant countries pay 10 percent.) The rice-wine also makes a great return, as does coal, of which there is a great quantity. . . . The silk which is produced in such abundance brings an immense return since they must pay 10 percent on it or more as on many other articles."

In Venice, where hundreds of small and midlevel merchants flourished, the manual was called the *tariffe,* an Arab word for "notification." A rare *tariffe* that has survived is the *Zibaldone da Canal,* written by anonymous Venetian businessmen in the 1300s and updated periodically well into the fifteenth century. Probably excerpted from dozens of sources, the book contains complicated arithmetical exercises using currency and products that a typical merchant could study in order to learn about his trade. An example that would interest an egg merchant poses this problem:

A group of merchants updates a merchant manual in this fifteenth-century drawing. Merchant manuals were filled with the latest information about medieval industries.

7 eggs are worth 5d [pennies]. How many can we have for 17d.? Now, remember that pennies are mentioned 2 times, and the first is the divisor, that is, 5. And then one ought to multiply 7 times 17, that makes 119, which one ought to divide in 5 parts. That comes to 23 and ⅘ eggs, and that is how many we can have for 17d. And by this rule do all similar calculations in this way.[56]

Other problems in the *Zibaldone da Canal* are incredibly complex. They are filled with conversions of weights, measures, currency, and languages and concern dozens of products such as olive oil, soap, honey, wool, and tin. Such a source was an invaluable tool to the traveling merchant, few of whom could hope to memorize the standards used in dozens of cities.

Merchant manuals also instructed readers on the uses for dozens of different spices and how best to judge the quality of perishable goods, including sugar, rice, and rhubarb. For example, the *Zibaldone da Canal* states that indigo from Baghdad, used to dye cloth blue, "ought to be of good, bright color outside and within, and light to the touch, and the pulp is light and when it is broken it ought to smell musty. Its proper color ought to be violet and dark within."[57]

Other manuals were useful for merchants who commanded sailing ships.

The *Book of the Sea,* a fifteenth-century manual from Flanders, contained valuable information on tides, depths, and dangers along specific sea routes. Italian merchant Francesco di Balduccio Pegolotti's manual *The Practice of Commerce* informs readers about dozens of towns the author had visited during his travels and provides information about the best products to purchase, weights and measures, taxes, and the price of local labor. Concerning tariffs, Pegolotti writes: "If you come with your merchandise to the port of Écluse [France] and do not unload, you can go on your way as you please, without unloading or paying any dues. But if you unload a single bale of your cargo, you will have to pay taxes on the whole of your goods still on the ship."[58]

Merchants who carried such informative books on long journeys could relax with other lessons that did not concern commercial interests. Legends and poetry were often interspersed with astrology lessons, Bible stories, and words to live by, such as "the excessive man cannot acquire great things that last long."[59] Merchant manuals were not always flawless, however, and some spread wildly inaccurate information. For example, merchants who wanted to stop nosebleeds were offered this bizarre advice in the *Zibaldone da Canal:*

[Take] the juice from the leaf of the pear, and vinegar, and the white of an egg, and the white

❧ THE MERCHANT'S COUNTING BOARD ❧

In the medieval era, merchants used a counting board, known as a Roman abacus, to keep track of funds and inventory. In his "Roman Arithmetic" Web article, John Durham explains that these boards were used for accounting—and for games:

[Medieval Italian merchants] calculated with an abacus. . . . [They] were . . . ruled boards or cloths on which the stones could be moved conveniently and quickly. . . . [Just] as modern computers are used both for calculation and gaming [these boards] became handy places to play games. Several of our most common games, including chess, checkers, and backgammon, are all played on versions of these boards. . . .

As to the details of how calculation was performed, the [Roman] numerals I, X, C, and M were usually represented by pebbles on the lines, while V, L, and D were represented by pebbles in the spaces between the lines (the lines were probably called "digitus"—modern "digit.") . . .

Used in this way, the abacus and Roman numerals were very efficient for ordinary commercial work, and could easily be adapted to handle fractions. . . .

The classical Roman word for what we call today by the term "abacus" was "tabula," and the counters which moved on it were called "calculi." Obviously the words *calculus* and *table* (in modern usage) somewhat reflect the ancient association of these terms with mathematics.

earth from the furriers, and the flour that flies from the wall of the mills, and the dung of an ass. Mix all these things together thoroughly, and put the mixture on the top of the head, and the forehead, and leave it there for 2 or 3 hours, and the blood will be well stanched. [60]

SHARING KNOWLEDGE

Merchant manuals were a limited source of knowledge in other ways, as they were often outdated by the time a single copy of the book was painstakingly reproduced by a scribe. For example, the price of pepper and gold went up or down almost daily when ships wrecked, kings were overthrown, or currency values fluctuated. In addition, because fashions quickly changed, a merchant buying a huge load of sable might find that this fur was unexpectedly shunned by the nobility who suddenly preferred lynx.

Since the greatest wealth went to those who stayed ahead of market demands, groups of merchants developed information networks to keep one another informed. In Tuscany, close-knit groups of traders circulated a sort of economic bulletin that contained information about the latest trends in art, fashion, religions, and business ventures, along with news of the day from distant shores. Favier describes the usefulness of these bulletins:

The well-informed negotiator would know the right moment to sell cloth of gold from Lucca, alabasters from England, [paintings of the] Virgin of the Seven Sorrows or a Mystic Marriage of St. Catherine. The agent in Paris would have been congratulated for predicting in his letters to his

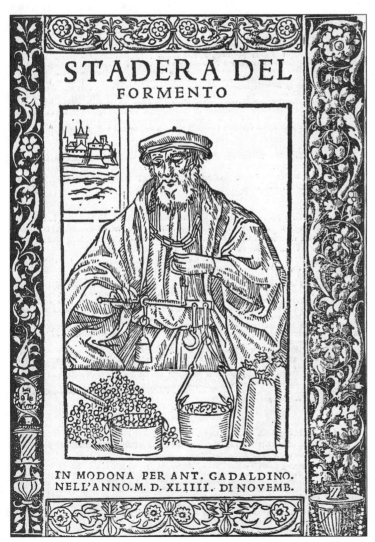

STADERA DEL
FORMENTO

IN MODONA PER ANT. GADALDINO.
NELL'ANNO.M. D. XLIIII. DI NOVEMB.

The cover of a medieval bulletin shows a merchant using weights and measures. Such bulletins were circulated to help keep merchants informed of new trends.

employers in Florence . . . that the probable peace and a possible alliance between France and England would come about only if sealed by a royal marriage. If the king of England was going to marry a French princess there would be great festivities: better to stock up in Paris with jewels than with weapons.[61]

Such communication methods not only contributed to the education of the young merchant but also undoubtedly helped large companies maintain an edge over competitors. In the quest for business knowledge, the bulletins, manuals, abacus schools, and universities that merchants used established a basis for secular education and public information that had been missing in previous centuries. As merchants pursued facts, data, and instructions about their world in order to make more money, the influence of the schools they supported broke the monopoly that the church had previously held over education. In this way the training, education, and information of the commercial revolution had a lasting impact on society.

CHAPTER 5

BUYING RESPECT

Medieval merchants were able to reap great profits buying and selling a diverse array of products. They were considered sinners in the eyes of God, however, by the powerful Christian church and many members of society. By living outside of the three divinely ordained orders of peasants, nobility, and clergy, merchants faced discrimination because they enriched themselves rather than working for the common good. It was said that merchants were not producing tangible products but were reselling the work of someone else for profit. Although merchants faced considerable risks obtaining merchandise that the clergy, nobility, and peasants demanded, they were nonetheless considered leeches who lived off the toil of others. The matter was aggravated when merchants became moneylenders who charged interest on their loans. This was regarded as the sin of usury, con-demned in the New Testament by Jesus who said, "lend [and] expecting nothing in return." [62]

Theologians took this one step further, equating usury with theft and advocating severe punishment for moneylenders. In 1215, the official emissary of the pope, Robert de Courçon, established a council to eliminate usury from the Christian world. Subsequently, in 1274, the governing body of the church, the Second Council of Lyons, gave communities three months to expel all usurers from their territories. The reasoning behind this drastic edict is explained in "Medieval Merchant Culture": "The objection to the presence of commerce . . . in early medieval times was spearheaded by the clergy, who thundered against the sinful nature of their calling. No sin was worse than that of the usurer, no activity more repugnant to the Lord." [63] The problem with such attitudes from

A sixteenth-century painting depicts a group of greedy merchants counting their money.

the merchant's point of view was that without the ability to borrow money or lend to others, economic stagnation would develop, leading to poverty. As fourteenth-century professor Benvenuto da Imola stated, "He who practiseth usury goeth to hell, and he who practiseth it not tendeth to destitution."[64]

FULL RESTITUTION

Fear of hell was very real for medieval merchants, many of whom routinely risked death from disease, bandits, accidents, and other threats. The dread of the inevitable judgment day was heightened considerably after the Second Council of Lyons refused Christian burial to usurers. It was believed that without Christian burial, the souls of the merchants were condemned to hell. This ban included one condition, however. Usurers could make amends for their sins by promising to return the money earned. As the Second Council wrote:

> [Ecclesiastical] burial is . . . to be refused until full restitution has been made as far as the usurer's means allow, or until a pledge has been given of fitting restitution. This pledge is to be given to those to whom restitution is due, if they themselves or others who can receive for them are present. If they are absent, the pledge is to be given to the local ordinary or his vicar or the rector of the parish where the testator [maker of the will] lives.[65]

Fearing an eternity in hell, medieval merchants like this man sometimes bequeathed their fortunes to their former customers.

Under these circumstances, the heirs of the testator could receive the bulk of their inheritance only after restitution was made to the usurer's former customers. To find the purported victims, the heirs asked the town council to send a crier into the streets. The crier rang a bell and shouted to all passersby that the merchant had died and his customers were entitled to a portion of his estate. These people appeared before a commission of monks who divided up the money.

This system was fraught with complications and corruption, however. The act of finding the borrowers with town criers was slow and often attracted dishonest people who falsely claimed that they were victims of the usurer. The monks had little interest in this duty and oftentimes simply kept the funds for themselves. In any case, because the laws were hard to enforce, restitution was left up to the conscience of the heirs, who often passed the task down to the next generation in their wills. In some cases, however, merchants left precise names and figures. In other cases, according to Armando Sapori in *The Italian Merchant in the Middle Ages,* "the bishop took an active part. He seized the dead man's account books and decided . . . how much had to be donated, over and above that which had been bequeathed to foundations, in an attempt to keep the soul of the de-

ceased from being engulfed in the eternal pit of Hell." [66]

The church would sometimes justify the seizure of the entire fortune of an extremely wealthy merchant by accusing the testator of sacrilegious behavior. Monks called inquisitors of heretical depravity might accuse a merchant of having questioned the sanctity of the church or preaching other blasphemous ideas during his life. In such cases the entire estate was confiscated by the church.

GIVING TO THE CHURCH

To avoid such ruinous incidents, merchants often sought to buy the respect of the church more directly by contributing to churches, monasteries, and priests. For example, many individuals set up a chantry, an endowment to one or more priests to say or sing Mass for the soul of the endower.

Others maintained what was called "devotional philanthropy" by giving gifts in perpetuity to the church itself. In 1436, an unnamed linen merchant provided a payment to women of a Venice church to buy candles to be lit in prayer "for the souls of the dead and for the well-being of the living . . . and for the sustenance of the poor and infirm." [67]

Venetian merchants with greater means often provided lavish gifts to churches that would elicit the gratitude of the parishioners for years or

⚜ DIVINE MALEDICTION AGAINST USURERS ⚜

In 1274, the Second Council of Lyons, a church-governing body, issued an edict that, among other things, detailed harsh treatment for usurers. The following excerpt, from an edict preventing anyone from renting houses to usurers, is from the Web article "Second Council of Lyons—1274":

Wishing to close up the abyss of usury, which devours souls and swallows up property. . . . Since the less convenient it is for usurers to lend, the more their freedom to practice usury is curtailed, we ordain . . . as follows. Neither a college, nor other community, nor an individual person . . . may permit those . . . who practice usury or wish to do so, to rent houses for that purpose or to oc-

cupy rented houses or to live elsewhere. Rather, they must expel all such notorious usurers from their territories within three months, never to admit any such for the future. Nobody is to let houses to them for usury, nor grant them houses under any other title. Those indeed who act otherwise, if they are ecclesiastical persons, patriarchs, archbishops or bishops, are to know that they incur automatic suspension; lesser individual persons, excommunication, colleges or other communities, interdict. . . . Furthermore, if they are layfolk, they are to be restrained from such transgression through their ordinaries by ecclesiastical censure, all privileges ceasing.

even centuries. For example, in the early fourteenth century, Scaglia Tifi of Burgundy provided money in his wills for the construction of several chapels. In Venice, a merchant commissioned renowned painter Gentile Bellini to create a painting for the church of San Daniele. He also provided the church with one of the finest altars in Venice. Artist Palma Giovane was hired by a dealer in silks to create a painting called *The Assumption* on a wall of the church of San Zulian. Others paid for silver candlesticks, chandeliers, statues, crosses, processional banners, ceremonial swords,

and carvings of angels. Not all of these items were given for charitable purposes alone, however. As Richard Mackenney writes in *Tradesmen and Traders,* "Some of the objects carried in processions may well have served to advertise the excellence of the [merchant's] wares,"[68] which were produced and sold by family members long after the merchant had died.

WILLS AND HOPEFUL PAUPERS

While many merchants donated to the church, in medieval England making spiritual amends by granting funds

Merchants assist the poor and sick in this fifteenth-century fresco. Many merchants tried to secure a place in heaven by performing charitable acts.

to charity was a popular practice. This often meant donating to various hospitals and almshouses, where the homeless and indigent were cared for.

The donations were bequeathed in a number of ways. Wealthy merchants sometimes left money in their wills for the establishment of new charity institutions. For example, Robert Holme of York established an almshouse in the city in 1406. In the village of Hull, four small hospitals were funded by merchant trusts. In Crossbridge, John Ake left enough property to establish an almshouse that sheltered twenty-four destitute citizens. John Armstrong of Beverley set up a trust fund that donated twenty pounds annually to St. John the Baptist almshouse from rents on his property managed by his survivors. This was a huge sum equal to a master carpenter's salary if he worked six days a week for about four years.

It was also considered a selfless act of charity to leave money to prisons, which were often filled with indigent people who were jailed when they failed to pay their bills. Some merchants willed cash to individual prisons; others left gifts to the debtors themselves. For example, in the fifteenth century, William Chimney of York left two pence to each prisoner, while John Carre ordered that forty shillings be spent on drinks and meat that would be divided among prisoners.

Occasionally testators simply ordered that funds be handed out to those gathered at their funerals. Such decrees were guaranteed to draw large crowds, as Jenny Kermode writes in *Medieval Merchants:*

> [One] can imagine the spirit of anticipation which must have followed news of a prominent merchant's demise, bringing hopeful paupers crowding around his house. That, of course, was one of the intentions behind such doles: the attraction of as many individuals and their prayers as possible. [69]

CREATIVE CHARITY

The funeral giveaways often took care of hundreds of poor people, at least temporarily. When Beverley merchant John Brompton died in 1407, his largesse included distribution of the huge sum of eighteen pounds in cash at his funeral. Brompton also allocated ten pounds for bread to feed paupers. There were limits on such charity, however. Such bequests often specified that the money be spent only on people who lived in the merchant's ecclesiastical parish. Sometimes the distribution was even narrower. York merchant John Goddysbuk ordered that four pence be passed down to each pauper "in the lane where I live." [70]

Medieval merchants believed that the prayers of the poor would help them gain access to heaven, and there were those who wanted to be prayed for by thankful paupers for extended periods of time. These merchants ordered that their money be doled out for periods extending from five to ten years.

Other merchants were more creative when it came to making amends for their ostensible sins. Some testators left sums up to twenty-five pounds to unmarried women who needed dowries to attract husbands. John Tutbury hoped to improve the morals of young women by leaving one hundred shillings to be split among the "honest virgins" [71] of Hull. Not all merchants were concerned with virtue, however, and some tried to assuage their guilt after death. For example, Venetian merchant Amanliee d'Albrecht left a large sum of money to provide dowries for poor young women, "those that he had violated . . . if they could be found." [72]

Some merchants had grander visions to be carried out after their death. These men had the money and the means to make a lasting impact on medieval culture. Oftentimes these

❧ THE ESTEEM OF THE NUNNERY ☙

The sons of well-to-do merchants could gain respect by marrying into nobility. In London, the daughters of medieval merchants could acquire the admiration of society by becoming nuns, as Sylvia L. Thrupp writes in The Merchant Class of Medieval London (1300–1500):

The girls of merchant families were much attracted by the pleasantness of the monastic life and the high social esteem it enjoyed. Nunneries were founded for gentlewomen and seldom accepted the daughters of lesser tradesmen, yet London merchants' daughters were able to gain entrance to all the more fashionable houses in the south of England. There is no evidence of any parental objections. Although dowries were exacted and small annuities were necessary to buy them comforts, their fathers could find it cheaper to put girls into nunneries than to marry them. One mercer [trader in silk] offered his daughters £20 and a silver cup if they should marry, with the alternative of £10 and "a les Cuppe" if they should "entre in to Religion." But the dowries given ran as high as £100, and legacies of jewelry, fur, and furniture would follow. A draper with a daughter in the minster [monastery church] of Sheppey left £200, to provide her with an annuity of £5, or to be available as a lump sum for her advancement should she have any opportunity of becoming prioress [nun in charge of a priory].

contributions not only elevated the status of the merchant in the eyes of society but also helped the merchant trade itself. This was most often seen in endowments set aside for public works projects such as paving roads, improving buildings in marketplaces, and building bridges, granaries, and water supply systems. Such grants were valuable to the testator because the church openly encouraged such gifts, even prompting parishioners to pray for bridge and street builders, or "them that brigges and stretes makes."[73]

RETIRING TO THE COUNTRY MANOR

Public works projects helped merchants gain respect among church leaders and average citizens. The best method for a merchant to bolster his place in society, however, was through the acquisition of land. At a time when most lands were owned by the church or the nobility, a landowning merchant could not be ignored by the ruling classes of medieval society.

Merchants most often worked in cities, but the sons of successful businessmen were sometimes able to buy country estates equal in value to the most important landowners in the area. As Sylvia L. Thrupp writes in *The Merchant Class of Medieval London (1300–1500):*

> By settling down on their manors they stood to gain in status . . . for the head of the family was before long likely to be drawn into the influential circle that controlled the administration of the county. The strategic steps that assured a son's entry into the leisured landowning class required a patient watching of the land . . . markets and were probably all more or less motivated by social ambition.[74]

A medieval tapestry shows a wealthy merchant hunting on his country estate. Owning land helped merchants gain the respect of the ruling classes.

The estate was a place where the landed merchant could live like nobility, hunting, fishing, and throwing parties. Business still had to be conducted, however, and this task was often left to junior family members who remained in the city to oversee the family enterprise. In some cases, merchants simply wanted the manor only for status and had no interest in living there. Instead they put a manager in charge of the property while working full-time. London grocer Thomas Knolles was one such man. He owned an estate in Hertfordshire for forty years, but his grandson was the first to enjoy the life of a country squire. As Thrupp writes, Knolles "was in no mind to leave the city or see his wholesale business abandoned. He placed an agent in charge of the manor and cannily bred both his sons to trade. . . . Not until the third generation . . . did the heir retire to the country and move into the squirearchy."[75]

The integration of fishmongers and wool merchants into genteel society was never fully accomplished, however, as "Medieval Merchant Culture" explains:

The merchant, during this transitional period, had to contend for respect and honor with the nobility and the knighthood. The nobility cultivated a disdain for the petty details of moneymaking and money-saving, which were the domain of the merchant. The nobility prided themselves on their ability to spend, to be showy and magnanimous. These qualities were directly at odds with the careful attention to profit and loss which characterized the commercial man. By [the fourteenth century], however, the merchant class was very rich . . . and they held positions of power in civic government. But they never completely overcame the general contempt for the way in which they acquired their wealth.[76]

MARRIAGE AND SOCIAL STATUS

While the nobility might disdain the landholding merchant, such contempt was less likely to be held against one's own family members. Thus marriage into a noble family was the surest way to buy respect in the rigid social structure of the medieval era. And once a merchant was ennobled, he entered into a world of respect and privilege known only by a few in the Middle Ages. Nobles commanded companies of soldiers, participated in local and national governance, and made up the power structure of the church, acting as cardinals and even popes. They could also ennoble their sons and daughters, even those born out of wedlock. And businessmen who were ennobled could continue to act as

❧ ADVANTAGES OF NOBILITY ❧

The ultimate goal for most wealthy merchants was to become a member of the nobility. In Gold and Spices: The Rise of Commerce in the Middle Ages, *Jean Favier explains why this goal was so desirable to French merchants:*

The advantages of nobility were obvious to the businessman. With his fortune made and his position as a noble consolidated, he also acquired tax privileges and estates. The privileges that accompanied a jurisdiction [the power to interpret and apply the law] were not insignificant, acting as they did as protection from legal surprises. In a country where the judge in a civil court was above all an arbitrator, there was much advantage in being assured of the best judges and most favorable laws. The nobility, which forbade basic commerce and placed limits on the pursuit of business, would be seen as nothing less than the final goal, the crowning achievement. But it would be a mistake to evaluate nobility entirely in terms of material advantages: it is clear from the behavior of the press of people who sought entry to the ranks of the nobility that the prime advantage was social position and the esteem that went with it. The honor of being noble could not be measured, but it counted for much and many would seek it, regardless of the financial cost involved. After all, in business, it is worth something to make one's neighbor jealous.

merchants while selling their wares to only the wealthiest customers.

Marrying nobility was not easy, as the nobility closed ranks against outsiders. For example, in fifteenth-century London, only 6 percent of merchants married noblewomen, while 64 percent married women of equal social rank. It was more common for noblemen to marry the daughters of rich businessmen, especially in cases in which a squire was facing financial difficulties. Such a marriage, and the dowry paid by the bride's father, could help restore the noble's fortune.

Oftentimes, once such an alliance was made, members of the two families intermarried for generations.

The goal of marriage was not always advanced social standing, however. In Italy, where merchants and nobles were often one and the same, it was common for businessmen to use marriage as a way to reduce competition with rival companies. In these cases, merchants arranged marriages of their sons or daughters to the children of their competitors, thus forming an alliance between former adversaries.

PATRONS OF THE ARTS

After merchants had secured their futures by joining the ranks of nobility through marriage, they were able to curry favor with kings and other nobles by becoming patrons of the arts. This often involved hiring artists, musicians, and writers to produce works that sometimes became immortal.

Arts patronage was particularly prevalent in the later years of the Middle Ages. By the fifteenth century, the power of the church was waning as the secular knowledge of ancient Greece and Rome was rediscovered by European intellectuals. This also meant that the church-based prejudices against merchants were less important. Wealthy

An artist shows a model of a church to his patron. Merchants often curried favor with the upper echelons of medieval society by serving as patrons of the arts.

businessmen could join the ranks of princes and kings and lavish money upon artists as a way of gaining respect. As fifteenth-century Italian business-man Giovanni Ruccellai said: "The gift of spending well is a virtue."[77]

In Italy and France, successful merchants competed to give commissions to painters, poets, and philosophers. The church retained considerable power, and so commissions of paintings and statues usually had Christian themes. Dozens of creations were entitled *Madonna and Child, The Wise Men, Nativity,* and *Deposition from the Cross.* These works either were donated to funerary chapels, churches, and monasteries or decorated the estates of the merchants. Many of the works commissioned by merchants were produced by renowned artists such as Sandro Botticelli, Leonardo da Vinci, Jan van Eyck, and Michelangelo and may be seen today in the world's major museum collections.

The tastes of merchants even gave rise to portraiture, what was then a new style of painting. As Favier writes, having one's portrait painted by a fa-mous artist "placed the merchant on the same footing as the prince."[78]

A PLACE IN HEAVEN

While many merchants moved up the social ladder through arts patronage, marriage, or charitable donations, only a select few moved into higher society. Most merchants continued to struggle through difficult conditions to earn their money. It was the prerogative of most to pass most of their wealth along to their heirs. For example, in fifteenth-century London only about 12 percent of merchants bequeathed money to the poor in their wills. A meager 1.8 percent contributed to public works.

Despite the parsimony of the majority, some of those who did give made lasting contributions to society in the construction of buildings, roads, and bridges, and in the commission of works of art. Indeed, there was no better way to buy respect from society—and ensure oneself a guaranteed place in heaven—than to share the wealth made from the buying and selling of goods.

CHAPTER 6

MERCHANT BANKERS: BROKERS OF POWER

Although there are no precise figures, historians estimate that merchants eventually made up about 10 to 20 percent of the medieval population, with greater numbers concentrated in cities such as London, Venice, and Paris. While their numbers were small, together these people reordered medieval society, instituting a commercial revolution that permanently changed the lives of peasants, religious leaders, and the nobility.

While most merchants lived and died in relative obscurity, a few rose from humble origins to dominate many aspects of medieval life. These traders, sometimes known as "merchant princes," created empires. Their business practices were far different from the pack-carrying peddlers of the eleventh century who carted their dusty products from one market to the next on foot. The merchant princes sat in their offices, known as counting-houses, and conducted business on a global scale. Relying on homing pigeons and swift messengers that carried orders over land and sea, the merchants studied markets to eliminate competition, invested money abroad, hired and fired artisans who made products in cities thousands of miles away, and analyzed the political changes and rumors of war in Constantinople, Paris, and Bruges. They lent money to kings and popes, financed wars, and often controlled entire markets in vital products.

THE RISE OF THE MERCHANT PRINCE

The rise of the merchant to powerful positions was fueled by an increase in the general wealth in the late fourteenth century. At that time, the broad middle class of merchants split into two levels. The lower level comprised shopkeepers, local traders, and other merchants. The upper level, which controlled most of the wealth, were financiers, investors, and bankers.

Francesco di Marco Datini of Prato is a good example of a merchant who rose to the higher level. Datini moved to the home of the papal court, Avignon, as a fifteen-year-old merchant apprentice in 1350. He rose into the upper middle classes after thirty years of selling armor, cloth, religious articles, paintings, jewelry, and other goods. After making a comfortable living, Datini moved to Florence, where he used his savings to open a bank.

Branches in Pisa, Genoa, Barcelona, Valencia, Majorca, Bruges, and London soon followed. Although he was making a fortune in banking, he continued to work as a merchant, trading in gems, artwork, furs, fine silks, and other luxury items. Datini was able to maintain his widely dispersed business empire only through incredibly hard work. He penned every business letter himself and stayed at his desk for days at a time, sometimes sleeping only four hours a night in his office chair. As he wrote to a friend in the 1390s, "It is the ninth hour [nine o'clock at night] . . . and I

A medieval fresco shows a market busy with merchants selling and trading goods. Although small in numbers, merchants played a significant role in medieval society.

have not yet eaten nor drunk, and tomorrow I shall do the same." [79]

Datini and other successful merchant bankers worked long hours because in the high-risk world of banking, they needed to keep abreast of all

After thirty years of working as a merchant, Francesco di Marco Datini amassed enough of a fortune to open a bank.

aspects of their business. As Raymond de Roover writes in *Gresham on Foreign Exchange,* a successful merchant banker "required extensive knowledge of monetary standards, mint regulations, shipping charges and insurance rates, commercial practices, the credit standing of business firms in all parts of the world, the currents of trade, and, above all, 'the ebb and flow' of the exchange, that is to say, the pattern of seasonal fluctuations in the money market." [80]

BANKER TO THE POPE

It was imperative that medieval merchant bankers understand the complicated world of finance. Most also found it beneficial to stay out of the public eye and conduct business with discretion and prudence. This was something Florence banker Giovanni di Bicci de' Medici, born in 1360, well understood. When Medici was a young apprentice, he was aware that the powerful Albizzi banking family used their political connections to arrest, banish, excommunicate, and even execute their rivals. When Medici went into the banking business, he was careful not to offend the Albizzis. By operating behind the scenes, however, the merchant banker was able to build one of the greatest fortunes of the Middle Ages.

By the first years of the fifteenth century, Medici was a merchant who owned two wool workshops in Florence and was a member of the

☙ WHY MERCHANTS BECAME BANKERS ❧

With their knowledge of economics and their constant need to borrow money, it was natural that successful merchants would want to become bankers. This issue is explored by Meir Kohn in the Web article "Merchant Banking in the Medieval and Early Modern Economy":

Why did some merchants become merchant bankers? Often, it was a case of one thing leading to another. Large trading companies with permanent branches or correspondents in many places found it easy to transfer funds for other merchants, so becoming merchant bankers. Because of the delay between the time a merchant bank accepted funds in one place and the time it paid them in another, it necessarily became the recipient of a loan. In this way, remittance [sending of money to someone at a distance] provided a merchant bank with funds that it could in turn lend and so drew it into finance.

There was another reason why some merchants came to specialize in finance. Commerce, when successful, could generate enormous profits. As a successful merchant's wealth grew, he found it necessary to increasingly devote his time to managing his wealth. Opportunities for further investment in his own business were limited, and considerations of diversification made it anyhow undesirable. Good financial assets were hard to find. In many cases, the wealthy merchant's best alternative was to lend his capital—to become a financier. The move was an easy one as he would already, as a merchant, have been well versed in finance.

wool merchants' guild. His main interest was banking, however, and he was also a member of the Arte del Cambio, the bankers' guild. Although he preferred to operate behind the scenes, as Christopher Hibbert writes in *The House of Medici: Its Rise and Fall,* "rich merchants did not prosper without taking a share in the government."[81]

With this in mind, Medici took over as head of the Arte del Cambio in 1402, which also allowed him to become a member of the Florence city government. In this position he was able to direct profits to his bank by acting as a rent collector on homes, warehouses, and other properties owned by the city. This money was lent to reliable merchants who paid it back with interest. The business practices of Medici and his business partner Benedetto de' Bardi are described by Joseph and Frances Gies: "Giovanni and Benedetto pursued a business policy compounded by prudence, alertness, and thrift. They neither overpaid their employees nor lent money to doubtful clients. Profits of 10 percent did not discourage them, though they preferred to see 30 percent."[82]

With a reputation for prudence and conservatism, Medici became deeply involved in politics when his friend Baldassare Cossa wished to be appointed cardinal legate in Bologna. Medici purchased the position for Cossa by giving Pope Alexander V the sum of ten thousand ducats, an amount equal to a housemaid's salary for about four years. When Alexander died under mysterious circumstances in 1410, Cossa himself was named Pope John XXIII. Medici's venture into politics had paid off. The pope appointed Medici to collect and disburse papal funds, which allowed the banker to make a fortune handling the church's finances. As Hibbert writes, however, this was an unusual friendship:

> Cossa . . . was not at all the sort of man with whom a rather staid and provident banker might be expected to associate. Sensual, adventurous, unscrupulous and highly superstitious, Baldassare Cossa . . . had once been a pirate. When he decided to enter the Church it appeared . . . that he sought further adventure rather than the service of God.[83]

As the pope's banker, Medici's stature grew considerably in the bustling world of Florentine business. However,

Giovanni di Bicci de' Medici built one of the greatest fortunes of the Middle Ages as a merchant banker.

Medici began to regret his friendship with the pope, whose legitimacy had been challenged by two rival claimants to the papacy. In 1415 John was formally deposed and accused of heresy, tyranny, and grave moral offenses (which were probably exaggerated). Once again known as Baldassare Cossa, the deposed pope disguised himself as a peasant and fled to Austria with a crossbow over his shoulder for protection. Medici lost his job as the pope's banker to a rival bank. In 1420, however, the rival bank failed and was absorbed by Medici's financial institutions. During the next few years, Medici became an international banker at the forefront of European finance, opening banking offices in Rome, Geneva, Pisa, Bruges, and London.

As one of the wealthiest men in Europe, Medici gave freely to charity, was a patron of the arts, and graciously paid for city improvements from his own accounts. He was much beloved by average citizens because he often championed the causes of the poor against the aristocracy. On his deathbed in 1429, Medici passed along advice to his children that had served him well throughout his life:

> Be inoffensive to the rich and strong . . . while being consistently charitable to the poor and weak. Do not appear to give advice, but put your views forward discreetly in conversation. Be wary of going to the [seat of government]; wait to be summoned, and when you *are* summoned, do what you are asked to do and never display any pride should you receive a lot of votes. . . . Avoid litigation and political controversy, and always keep out of the public eye. [84]

SOVEREIGN LENDING

While Medici made his fortunes by befriending religious officials, other merchant bankers chose to lend money to kings and princes. This practice,

called sovereign lending, was particularly risky because if a prince or king defaulted on a loan, the merchant banker had no recourse but to fight him in a royal court—overseen by the sovereign himself. In addition, if the royal died, his heirs were not responsible for his debts. And in this age of rampant disease, palace revolutions, and warfare, few members of the royalty died of old age. While lending to nobles was risky, the possible profits encouraged some merchant bankers to make such loans.

A merchant banker could make a profit when lending to kings or princes in several ways. First, the merchant banker could lend his own money, or borrow money in his name and then lend it, to the sovereign to be repaid with interest. Alternatively, the merchant could lend money to the sovereign free of interest in exchange for favors. In such cases, merchant lenders were rewarded with access to markets. For example, the Peruzzi family of merchant bankers had fifteen branches across Europe and the Levant, and their banking empire was the largest in the world in the fourteenth century. In the 1340s, the Peruzzis lent the huge sum of £210,000 to English king Edward III to help pay for the Hundred Years' War against France. In exchange, they gained monopolistic access to the wool trade in England.

When Edward III did not pay the Peruzzis back as promised, their banking empire collapsed. This, in turn, had a major impact on the Florentine economy, plunging it into a depression known as the Great Crash.

"SPEAK, ACT, BE SILENT"

While bankruptcy was a risk that many sovereign lenders faced, French merchant Jacques Coeur discovered that trusted clients could not only ruin him financially but also put him in prison. Although Coeur was not as rich or powerful as the Peruzzis, he had become quite successful in the 1420s selling furs to nobility. His best customer was Duke Jean de Berry, who favored ermine, silver fox, and marten and who even decorated his horses with expensive fur trim. Coeur used the profits from his dealings with the nobleman and his court to fund a business that exported European sil-

⚜ PAYING FOR THE HUNDRED YEARS' WAR ⚜

The Hundred Years' War, which lasted from the mid-fourteenth to the mid-fifteenth centuries, was one of the most disruptive wars of the Middle Ages. Fought between England and France, the war was largely financed by merchant bankers who lent money to English king Edward III. In turn, the king granted rights and privileges to the merchants, as Milly McCloskey explains in the Web article "Medieval Merchants and Artisans":

Beginning with the end of the thirteenth century, certain German merchants . . . acted as credit bankers, lending [large] sums to the crown. . . . The most important loans were those made to Edward III. From 1338–1344 certain Hanseatic merchants lent him 44,000 pounds. For these sums the merchants received export licenses, reduced customs dues and the right to collect customs dues from other merchants. All told the sums Edward III borrowed to finance his war with France came to 330,250 pounds; 44,250 from Hanseatic merchants, 210,000 from Bardi and Peruzzi (Italian merchants and bankers) and 76,000 from an Englishman, William de la Pole. . . . When the Bardi and Peruzzi banks failed, the Hanseatic merchants . . . realized the risks they were taking by engaging in the business of credit, and gradually restricted their business to commercial enterprises. The foregoing makes it clear just how much influence the German merchants had acquired in England. Without their financial support, Edward III could not have waged war against France as effectively as he did. We could even speculate that the outcome of the war [with England defeating France] might have been different.

ver to China while importing gold to Europe from the East.

In the 1430s, Coeur was rich enough to curry favor with French king Charles VII by paying for the wedding of his son. He further ingratiated himself with Charles VII by paying to support the king's mistress, Agnes Sorel. The association with the king bred more success and Coeur quickly built a cloth empire, controlling every aspect of the business from the farming to the dyeing to the creation of the finished product. Coeur was able to further profit by building a paper mill that made high-quality paper from the discarded linen rags from his nearly three hundred factories.

Although he was one of the richest men in France and a friend to kings and nobles, Coeur preferred to remain out of the public eye, putting forth business propositions and letting his assistants execute them. His simple philosophy for success was illustrated in his motto: "Speak, act, be silent," [85] which was engraved on the central tower of his lavish château.

Coeur's ties to Charles VII were strengthened in 1439 when the king made the merchant the royal treasurer. In this capacity, Coeur reorganized the royal finances and established a gold standard that helped curtail dangerous fluctuations in the French currency. Ten years later, Charles prevailed over England in several battles of the Hundred Years' War, in part

with the help of Coeur, who lent the king nearly one ton of pure gold to build a professional army.

By this time Coeur was operating as an open pocketbook for the royal court. When the queen wanted a new dress, he gave her four hundred pounds. When the admiral of France wanted to construct a warship, Coeur lent him a huge sum of money. The merchant banker also handed out funds to bishops, bailiffs, royal lawyers, and other officials. In return, Coeur's customers often put up property as collateral. In some cases when the loans were not repaid, the lands were confiscated. In this way, the French merchant became an enemy to several powerful royals.

In 1451, Coeur was arrested and inexplicably accused of poisoning Agnes Sorel, who had died recently from complications of pregnancy. Although these charges were false, they were brought by courtiers who owed substantial sums to the merchant banker. After the arrest, Charles seized Coeur's extensive assets and used some of the money to continue military operations against the English. The Jacques Coeur page at the XENOPHON Group Web site discusses the trial that followed:

A trial was held, where the judges were among known merchant enemies of Jacques as well as various "royal commissioners" who had been granted "temporary"

Jacques Coeur stands trial in this engraving. As part of his sentence, the government seized his enormous assets.

possession of Jacques' forfeited estates. While the ridiculous poisoning charge was discredited (the originators, themselves, convicted for false witness in separate trials), many other offenses were injected: providing armor to the [enemy], coining fake money, kidnap-ping oarsmen for his galleys, [freeing] a Christian slave who had taken sanctuary on board one of his ships, committing extortion . . . and many more. [86]

Coeur, who remained in prison during his trial, was eventually found guilty and ordered confined until he paid a huge fine. This was impossible, since his assets had been seized. The former banker remained in jail until 1455 when he escaped to Rome, where he was received with honors by the pope. With his fortune gone, Coeur agreed to act as captain for a fleet of sixteen warships in a papal-sponsored war against the Turks. The next year, Coeur, once one of the most successful and wealthy merchant bankers of the late medieval period, died in battle at the age of sixty-one.

A MONOPOLY ON MINING

Despite the lessons of the Coeur debacle, merchant bankers continued to lend to royalty. While most suffered as a result, a few astute merchants were able to parlay their loans into some of the greatest fortunes in history. In Germany, for example, the powerful Fugger family was able to benefit significantly by lending money to several dukes and emperors.

The Fugger family had modest beginnings, with Hans Fugger importing raw cotton from Mediterranean ports by mule in the fourteenth century. By the end of the fifteenth century, however, his grandson, Jacob Fugger II, known as Jacob the Rich, owned extensive real estate, merchant fleets, and lavish mansions throughout Europe. He was able to obtain these riches through his connections with Duke Sigismund of the Tyrol in present-day Austria.

Duke Sigismund was the son of a cash-poor noble known as Frederick with the Empty Pockets, and the duke was equally pressed for funds. Sigismund did have something of value, however: the right to charge a tax, or royalty, on all copper and silver mined in the Schwaz region of his kingdom. As was typical of the nobility, the duke did not want to wait for the money to trickle in as the ore was mined but wanted large amounts of cash immediately. As Joseph and Frances Gies write, the duke was "fond of luxury . . . addicted to fighting with his Swiss neighbors, [and

Known as Jacob the Rich, Jacob Fugger II owned real estate, merchant fleets, and lavish mansions throughout Europe.

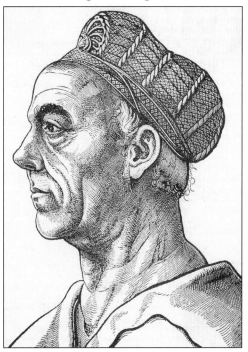

was] . . . trapped in the familiar princely vicious cycle of successive borrowings against future royalties."[87]

Sensing a monumental business opportunity, Jacob Fugger shrewdly advanced the huge sum of 150,000 florins to the duke in exchange for all metal-ore royalties from his mines until the loan was repaid. When the duke abdicated his throne to his cousin Emperor Maximilian I in 1490, the emperor decided to honor his cousin's debts to Fugger because the sovereign wanted to borrow even more money. Like the duke before him, Maximilian had little access to funds and little knowledge of finances, and he loved to fight wars. Over the next several years, Fugger loaned Maximilian money under conditions highly favorable to the merchant banker. Finally, Fugger demanded that he be granted a monopoly over all copper mining throughout Germany. Needing money, Maximilian had little choice but to accept the terms.

"FURTHERING THE FUGGER TRADE"

Using the funds from Maximilian's mines, Fugger expanded his operations to take control of copper mines in Russia, Slovakia, and elsewhere. Moreover, the merchant was not above utilizing marriage in order to extend his powers. In Hungary, Johann Thurzo had a controlling interest in the copper mines, so Fugger arranged to have two members of his family marry two members of Thurzo's family. These arranged marriages were simply part of doing business with Jacob, who expected family members to help, as he said, in the "furthering of the Fugger trade."[88]

While taking control of the precious metals market, Fugger remained a merchant, extending his financial reach to dominate the Hanseatic markets in wax, furs, spices, glass, cloth, and metal goods. Fugger and his family partners were able to do this through shrewd business practices, as Philippe Dollinger writes in *The German Hansa*:

> [Hansa merchants] seem to have regarded the Fuggers principally as bankers, engaged in transferring funds. . . . Their blindness can be explained perhaps by the cunning of Jacob Fugger. Acting on good advice, he concealed his real intentions, doing business through Hanseatic . . . correspondents, buying their complicity where necessary, retreating when it seemed advisable.[89]

While Jacob the Rich treated his competition harshly, he was equally as hard on his family, on whom he depended to oversee his empire. Before he would reveal his business practices to his nephews, for example, he made

᥎ MEDIEVAL BANKS ᥍

Medieval bankers were often powerful merchants who controlled large sectors of the economy and often manipulated government and religious policy by lending to kings and popes. However, as Raymond de Roover writes in The Rise and Decline of the Medici Bank, *medieval bankers ran their operations from simple, modest offices:*

It would be a grievous mistake to have an exaggerated idea of the size of medieval banks and to picture them as giant institutions doing business in office buildings with marble lobbies and rows of windows behind which a crowd of employees operate machines and manipulate papers. In reality medieval bankers transacted their business in small offices adorned with a bank, or counter, a few desks, and, in the rear, the abacus on which the bookkeeper made his computations by casting his counters. It was exceptional for more than half-a-dozen clerks to be working in such a countingroom.

A fifteenth-century fresco shows a medieval bank, which were typically very small and modest.

them swear on a Bible and sign a contract that read, in part:

> [The nephews] are faithfully bound to be true and obedient in all things [and] to hold the business in complete secrecy and tell no one. . . . [They] shall do nothing but what I command and give them permission to do. And if I direct one or all of them to do something, and afterward recall it to myself, they shall not dispute it. [90]

That Fugger valued secrecy is no surprise, and he used a series of spies and informers to collect intelligence on economic and political events throughout Europe. He developed a network of well-paid agents inside royal courts and chancelleries that furnished him with intelligence unknown to others. It was delivered to Fugger by his private courier service. Information that was of little use to Fugger was published in newsletters that were circulated among other merchant bankers. Valuable business and political information was held in the utmost secrecy and acted upon when it was beneficial to the banker.

A NEW WORLD BECKONS

As the Middle Ages drew to a close, the world of bankers and merchants changed rapidly. In 1492, Christopher Columbus, son of Genoese wool merchants, discovered the New World, a land of unimaginable riches. When he landed in the Caribbean, Columbus had been searching for a shorter sea route to India so that spice traders could cut their costs. Although the focus of economics and trade shifted to North America in the following centuries, it was the merchants of the Middle Ages who laid the foundation for this bridge to the New World. From the dusty-footed peddlers to the wealthy bankers, the growth and progress of European civilization depended in a large part on men and women in search of profit.

NOTES

INTRODUCTION: THE RISE OF THE MERCHANT CLASS

1. Gerhard Rempel, "Guilds and Commerce," Western New England College, http://mars.acnet.wnec.edu/~grempel/courses/wc1/lectures/24guilds.html.
2. Quoted in Urban Tigner Holmes Jr., *Daily Living in the Twelfth Century.* Madison: University of Wisconsin Press, 1952, pp. 143–44.
3. Robert S. Lopez and Irving W. Raymond, eds., *Medieval Trade in the Mediterranean World.* New York: Columbia University Press, 2001, p. 51.
4. "Medieval Merchant Culture," Decameron Web, www.brown.edu/Departments/Italian_Studies/dweb/society/structure/merchant_cult.shtml.

CHAPTER ONE: TRAVELING THE TRADE ROUTES

5. Francesco di Balduccio Pegolotti, "The Road to China: A Merchant's Guide," Houghton Mifflin College, http://college.hmco.com/history/west/mosaic/chapter9/source273.html.
6. Quoted in Olivia Remie Constable, *Housing the Stranger in the Mediterranean World.* Cambridge: Cambridge University Press, 2003, p. 89.
7. Quoted in Constable, *Housing the Stranger in the Mediterranean World,* p. 95.
8. Quoted in Lopez and Raymond, *Medieval Trade in the Mediterranean World,* pp. 31–32.
9. Joseph Gies and Frances Gies, *Merchants and Moneymen.* New York: Thomas Y. Crowell, 1972, p. 30.
10. Robert Bargrave, and Michael G. Brennan, ed., *The Travel Diary of Robert Bargrave, Levant Merchant.* London: Hakluyt Society, 1999, p. 54.
11. Jean Favier, *Gold and Spices: The Rise of Commerce in the Middle Ages.* New York: Holmes & Meier, 1998, p. 32.
12. Quoted in Iris Origo, *The Merchant of Prato.* New York: Alfred A. Knopf, 1957, p. 59.
13. Quoted in E. Gee Nash, *The Hansa: Its History and Romance.* London: John Lane, The Bodley Head, 1929, p. 66.
14. Favier, *Gold and Spices,* pp. 11–12.
15. Quoted in Favier, *Gold and Spices,* p. 12.
16. Edwin S. Hunt, *The Medieval Super-Companies.* Cambridge: Cambridge University Press, 1994, pp. 65–66.
17. Quoted in Origo, *The Merchant of Prato,* p. 68.
18. Bargrave and Brennan, *The Travel Diary of Robert Bargrave,* p. 174.

CHAPTER TWO: MERCHANTS AT MARKETS AND FAIRS

19. Quoted in Gies and Gies, *Merchants and Moneymen,* p. 29.
20. Gies and Gies, *Merchants and Moneymen,* p. 29.
21. Quoted in Lopez and Raymond, *Medieval Trade in the Mediterranean World,* p. 69.
22. Lucian, "Medieval Sourcebook: The Great Fair at Thessalonica, Mid 12th Century," *Medieval Sourcebook,* Fordham University Center for Medieval Studies, 1997. www.fordham.edu/halsall/source/thess-fair.html.
23. "Introduction to Late Medieval English Mercantile Narratives and Gendered Mercantile Concerns," University of Delaware English Department, www.english.udel.edu/dean/cv/gastdiss.html.
24. Quoted in "Medieval Sourcebook: Accounts of Medieval Fairs and Markets, c. 998–1250," *Medieval Sourcebook,* Fordham University Center for Medieval Studies, November 9, 1999. www.fordham.edu/halsall/source/1250medfairs.html.
25. Quoted in G.G. Coulton, *Social Life in Britain: From the Conquest to the Reformation.* Cambridge: Cambridge University Press, 1938, 332.
26. Quoted in Coulton, *Social Life in Britain,* p. 324.
27. Quoted in Coulton, *Social Life in Britain,* p. 327.
28. Gies and Gies, *Merchants and Moneymen,* p. 78.
29. Gies and Gies, *Merchants and Moneymen,* p. 78.
30. Quoted in "Medieval Sourcebook: Accounts of Medieval Fairs and Markets."
31. Peter Spufford, *Power and Profit: The Merchant in Medieval Europe.* New York: Thames & Hudson, 2002, pp. 146–47.

CHAPTER THREE: MERCHANT GUILDS

32. Georges Renard, *Guilds in the Middle Ages.* New York: Augustus M. Kelly, 1968, p. 27.
33. Quoted in Charles Gross, *The Gild Merchant.* New York: Oxford University Press, 1964, p. 8.
34. Quoted in Lopez and Raymond, *Medieval Trade in the Mediterranean World,* p. 129.
35. Quoted in Lopez and Raymond, *Medieval Trade in the Mediterranean World,* p. 128.
36. Rempel, "Guilds and Commerce."
37. Lopez and Raymond, *Medieval Trade in the Mediterranean World,* p. 21.
38. Quoted in Rempel, "Guilds and Commerce."
39. Renard, *Guilds in the Middle Ages,* p. 43.
40. Quoted in Gross, *The Gild Merchant,* p. 32.
41. Quoted in Gross, *The Gild Merchant,* p. 33.

42. Quoted in "Medieval Sourcebook: Southampton Guild Organization, 14th Century," *Medieval Sourcebook,* Fordham University Center for Medieval Studies, 1996. www.fordham.edu/halsall/source/guildsthhmptn.html.

43. Quoted in "Medieval Sourcebook: Southampton Guild Organization."

44. Renard, *Guilds in the Middle Ages,* p. 22.

45. Renard, *Guilds in the Middle Ages,* pp. 24–25.

46. Paul Schulz, "The Hanseatic League (Hansa)," GAFA—German American Fellowship Association of MN, April 2001. www.gafa.org/published_articles/21-Hanseatic_League/hanseatic_league.htm.

47. Nash, *The Hansa: Its History and Romance,* pp. 112–13.

CHAPTER FOUR: EDUCATING AND TRAINING THE MERCHANT CLASS

48. Favier, *Gold and Spices,* p. 54.

49. Quoted in Benjamin Z. Kedar, *Merchants in Crisis.* New Haven, CT: Yale University Press, 1976, p. 38.

50. Quoted in J.J. O'Connor and E.F. Robertson, "Leonardo Pisano Fibonacci," University of St Andrews, October 1998. www-groups.dcs.st-and.ac.uk/~history/Mathematicians/Fibonacci.html.

51. Quoted in Holmes Jr., *Daily Living in the Twelfth Century,* pp. 82–83.

52. Quoted in Holmes Jr., *Daily Living in the Twelfth Century,* p. 81.

53. Quoted in Holmes Jr., *Daily Living in the Twelfth Century,* p. 81.

54. Origo, *The Merchant of Prato,* p. 77.

55. John E. Dotson, ed., *Merchant Culture in the Fourteenth Century: The Zibaldone da Canal.* Binghamton, NY: Medieval & Renaissance Texts & Studies, 1994, p. 23.

56. Quoted in Dotson, *Merchant Culture in the Fourteenth Century,* p. 38.

57. Quoted in Dotson, *Merchant Culture in the Fourteenth Century,* p. 139.

58. Quoted in Favier, *Gold and Spices,* p. 65.

59. Quoted in Dotson, *Merchant Culture in the Fourteenth Century,* p. 164.

60. Quoted in Dotson, *Merchant Culture in the Fourteenth Century,* pp. 150–51.

61. Favier, *Gold and Spices,* p. 67.

CHAPTER FIVE: BUYING RESPECT

62. "Luke 6," Bible.com, http://bibleontheweb.com/Bible.asp.

63. "Medieval Merchant Culture," Decameron Web.

64. Quoted in Coulton, *Social Life in Britain,* p. 343.

65. "Second Council of Lyons—1274," All Catholic Church Ecumenical Councils. www.piar.hu/councils/ecum14.htm.

66. Armando Sapori, *The Italian Merchant in the Middle Ages.* New York: W.W. Norton, 1970, p. 27.

67. Quoted in Richard Mackenney, *Tradesmen and Traders.* London: Croom Helm, 1987, p. 61.

68. Mackenney, *Tradesmen and Traders,* p. 62.
69. Jenny Kermode, *Medieval Merchants.* Cambridge: Cambridge University Press, 1998, p. 148.
70. Quoted in Kermode, *Medieval Merchants,* p. 149.
71. Quoted in Kermode, *Medieval Merchants,* p. 149.
72. Quoted in Sapori, *The Italian Merchant in the Middle Ages,* p. 26.
73. Quoted in Kermode, *Medieval Merchants,* p. 151.
74. Sylvia L. Thrupp, *The Merchant Class of Medieval London (1300–1500).* Chicago: University of Chicago Press, 1948, p. 230.
75. Thrupp, *The Merchant Class of Medieval London,* p. 230.
76. "Medieval Merchant Culture," Decameron Web.
77. Quoted in Favier, *Gold and Spices,* p. 359.
78. Favier, *Gold and Spices,* p. 361.

CHAPTER SIX: MERCHANT BANKERS: BROKERS OF POWER
79. Quoted in Origo, *The Merchant of Prato,* p. 97.

80. Raymond de Roover, *Gresham on Foreign Exchange.* Cambridge: Harvard University Press, 1949, p. 166.
81. Christopher Hibbert, *The House of Medici: Its Rise and Fall.* New York: Perennial, 2003, p. 32.
82. Gies and Gies, *Merchants and Moneymen,* p. 241.
83. Hibbert, *The House of Medici,* p. 34.
84. Quoted in Hibbert, *The House of Medici,* p. 41.
85. Quoted in Gies and Gies, *Merchants and Moneymen,* p. 225.
86. Société de l'Oriflamme, "Jacques Coeur," XENOPHON Group, June 17, 2002. www.xenophon group.com/montjoie/j_coeur.htm.
87. Gies and Gies, *Merchants and Moneymen,* p. 276.
88. Quoted in Jacob Strieder, "Chapter 10—The Fuggers," Bunker Consulting Group, 1999. www.bunker co.com/masters/chap10.
89. Philippe Dollinger, *The German Hansa.* Stanford, CA: Stanford University Press, 1970, p. 318.
90. Quoted in Gies and Gies, *Merchants and Moneymen,* p. 283.

FOR FURTHER READING

BOOKS

James Barter, *A Travel Guide to Medieval Constantinople*. San Diego: Lucent Books, 2003. A visitors' guide to Constantinople in 1024—including what to see, where to stay, and what to eat—that would have proved useful to any merchant traveling to the city that lay at the center of medieval commerce.

Tehmina Bhote, *Medieval Feasts and Banquets: Food, Drink, and Celebration in the Middle Ages*. New York: Rosen, 2004. Provides insight into the food products made available by merchants along with the feasting and drinking experienced by the richest citizens of the medieval world.

Ruth Dean and Melissa Thomson, *Women of the Middle Ages*. San Diego: Lucent Books, 2003. Explores the roles—including skilled workers, artisans, and merchants—taken on by women during the medieval period.

Priscilla Galloway, *Archers, Alchemists, and 98 Other Medieval Jobs You Might Have Loved or Loathed*. New York: Annick, 2003. Occupations of the Middle Ages, many of them associated with medieval merchants and the goods they bought and sold.

Kathryn Hinds, *Life in the Middle Ages: The City*. New York: Benchmark Books, 2001. An overview of city life where commerce was the main attraction in the medieval era.

WEB SITES

Medieval English Genealogy (www. medievalgenealogy.org.uk/sitemap. shtml). This comprehensive, useful site offers a wide range of links to medieval documents concerning the production, sale, and regulation of goods; guild records; and calendars of medieval market activity. Includes facsimiles of primary source material accompanied by clear discussion.

Medieval Sourcebook (www.ford ham.edu/halsall/sbook.html). The Fordham University Center for Medieval Studies provides this Web site with links to hundreds of primary documents about medieval life. Includes maps and bibliographies.

The Merchant's Realm (http:// emuseum.mankato.msus.edu/ history/middleages/merchant.html) Sponsored by the University of Minnesota's EMuseum project, this site aimed at students describes the medieval merchant's trade and travel, town life, and apprenticeship, and offers useful links to broader topics on the Middle Ages.

WORKS CONSULTED

BOOKS

Robert Bargrave, and Michael G. Brennan, ed., *The Travel Diary of Robert Bargrave, Levant Merchant.* London: Hakluyt Society, 1999. An invaluable journal of life as a traveling English merchant in Constantinople, Italy, and Spain.

Norman F. Cantor, *The Civilization of the Middle Ages.* New York: Harper-Collins, 1993. First published in 1963, this scholarly volume explores the evolution of European society against the backdrop of wars, religious upheavals, and intellectual and cultural revolutions.

E.M. Carus-Wilson, *Medieval Merchant Venturers.* London: Methuen, 1954. A series of essays concerning the English cloth and wool trade during the Middle Ages.

Olivia Remie Constable, *Housing the Stranger in the Mediterranean World.* Cambridge: Cambridge University Press, 2003. A fascinating study of lodging, trade, and travel in the Middle Ages in the Levant and European countries.

G.G. Coulton, *Social Life in Britain: From the Conquest to the Reformation.* Cambridge: Cambridge University Press, 1938. Descriptions of daily life, customs, beliefs, religion, and war taken from diaries, journals, and books written during the Middle Ages.

Raymond de Roover, *Gresham on Foreign Exchange.* Cambridge: Harvard University Press, 1949. An essay on medieval English mercantilism based on the writings of Sir Thomas Gresham, a financial adviser to royalty.

———, *The Rise and Decline of the Medici Bank.* Cambridge: Harvard University Press, 1963. A scholarly study of the Florentine bank that dominated European commerce from 1397 to 1494.

Philippe Dollinger, *The German Hansa.* Stanford, CA: Stanford University Press, 1970. A study of the league of merchants who dominated trade in northern Europe for nearly five centuries.

John E. Dotson, ed., *Merchant Culture in the Fourteenth Century: The Zibaldone da Canal.* Binghamton, NY: Medieval & Renaissance Texts & Studies, 1994. A merchant's guide with a gazetteer, tips on currency, mathematics, and other necessary information written by anonymous Venetian businessmen in the 1300s.

Carolly Erickson, ed., *The Records of Medieval Europe.* Garden City, NY: Anchor, 1973. Ancient written words divided into early, middle, and late periods of the Middle Ages concerning government, commerce, religions, public life, literature, and the social order.

Jean Favier, *Gold and Spices: The Rise of Commerce in the Middle Ages.* New York: Holmes & Meier, 1998. The political, social, moral, and economic environment in Europe during the late Middle Ages when the continent was transformed from a feudal to a capitalistic society.

Joseph Gies and Frances Gies, *Merchants and Moneymen.* New York: Thomas Y. Crowell, 1972. The commercial revolution in Europe between 1000 and 1500 based on the written records left by merchants from England, Italy, and elsewhere.

Charles Gross, *The Gild Merchant.* New York: Oxford University Press, 1964. First published in 1890, this book traces the rise and fall of merchant guilds in Europe using an abundance of medieval source documents.

Christopher Hibbert, *The House of Medici: Its Rise and Fall.* New York: Perennial, 2003. A reprint of the 1974 book that explores the Florentine merchant banking family and their wealth, power, and contributions to medieval culture.

Urban Tigner Holmes Jr., *Daily Living in the Twelfth Century.* Madison: University of Wisconsin Press, 1952. A book about medieval life based on the observations of thirteenth-century Italian, French, Spanish, and English authors.

Edwin S. Hunt, *The Medieval Super-Companies.* Cambridge: Cambridge University Press, 1994. The history, business practices, successes, and failures of the Peruzzi family company that operated in Florence from 1300 to 1343.

Benjamin Z. Kedar, *Merchants in Crisis.* New Haven, CT: Yale University Press, 1976. A study of Genoese and Venetian merchants and their business practices during a devastating fourteenth-century economic depression.

Jenny Kermode, *Medieval Merchants.* Cambridge: Cambridge University Press, 1998. A scholarly study of merchant society, politics, business, and culture in the English towns of York, Beverley, and Hull in the late Middle Ages.

Robert S. Lopez and Irving W. Raymond, eds., *Medieval Trade in the Mediterranean World.* New York: Columbia University Press, 2001. A valuable collection of source documents, written during the Middle Ages, dealing with all aspects of medieval mercantilism.

Richard Mackenney, *Tradesmen and Traders.* London: Croom Helm, 1987. A study of the guilds in Venice and the rest of Europe in the years between 1250 and 1650.

E. Gee Nash, *The Hansa: Its History and Romance.* London: John Lane, The Bodley Head, 1929. A colorful history of the Hanseatic League, the mercantile company formed by German towns in the late Middle Ages.

Iris Origo, *The Merchant of Prato.* New York: Alfred A. Knopf, 1957. A biography based on the writings of the traveling merchant Francesco di Marco Datini who worked out of Prato, Italy, in the late fourteenth and early fifteenth centuries.

Marco Polo, *The Travels of Marco Polo.* New York: Orion, 1958. The late thirteenth-century and early fourteenth-century writings of the Italian explorer, who was one of the first Europeans to travel across Asia.

———, *The Book of Marco Polo.* 2 vols. Trans. and ed. Col. Sir Henry Yule. New York: Charles Scribner's Sons, 1903. Polo's famous medieval descriptions of the marvelous lands east of the Mediterranean and his experiences in the court of Kublai Khan inspired merchants and explorers and shaped Europeans' view of Asia for centuries.

Georges Renard, *Guilds in the Middle Ages.* New York: Augustus M. Kelly, 1968. First published in 1918, this work examines the various types of guilds, their administration, their goals, and their decay in the later medieval period.

Armando Sapori, *The Italian Merchant in the Middle Ages.* New York: W.W. Norton, 1970. The lives, culture, and societies of merchants from Venice, Genoa, Pisa, and elsewhere in Italy.

Peter Spufford, *Power and Profit: The Merchant in Medieval Europe.* New York: Thames & Hudson, 2002. An informative examination of trade in the Middle Ages and its influence on culture and society, illustrated with hundreds of maps, period paintings, and pictures.

Sylvia L. Thrupp, *The Merchant Class of Medieval London (1300–1500).* Chicago: University of Chicago Press, 1948. An in-depth study of London merchants including their population, governmental participation, standards of living, conduct of life, and contributions to society.

INTERNET SOURCES

John Durham, "Roman Arithmetic," Math Forum, December 16, 1996. http://mathforum.org/epigone/math-history-list/walcronthah/19961216132947101.AAA929@FHSUVM.FHSU.EDU.

"Introduction to Late Medieval English Mercantile Narratives and Gendered

Mercantile Concerns," University of Delaware English Department, www.english.udel.edu/dean/cv/gastdiss.html.

Meir Kohn, "Merchant Banking in the Medieval and Early Modern Economy," February 1999. www.dartmouth.edu/~mkohn/99-05.pdf.

Lucian, "Medieval Sourcebook: The Great Fair at Thessalonica, Mid 12th Century," *Medieval Sourcebook,* Fordham University Center for Medieval Studies, 1997. www.fordham.edu/halsall/source/thess-fair.html.

"Luke 6," Bible.com, http://bibleontheweb.com/Bible.asp.

Milly McCloskey, "Medieval Merchants and Artisans," Stefan's Florilegium, March 5, 2001. www.florilegium.org/files/COMMERCE/Med-Merchants-CA.text.

"Medieval Merchant Culture," Decameron Web. www.brown.edu/Departments/Italian_Studies/dweb/society/structure/merchant_cult.shtml.

"Medieval Sourcebook: Accounts of Medieval Fairs and Markets, c. 998–1250," *Medieval Sourcebook,* Fordham University Center for Medieval Studies, November 9, 1999. www.fordham.edu/halsall/source/1250medfairs.html.

"Medieval Sourcebook: Southampton Guild Organization, 14th Century," *Medieval Sourcebook,* Fordham Uni-versity Center for Medieval Studies, 1996. www.fordham.edu/halsall/source/guild-sthhmptn.html.

J.J. O'Connor and E.F. Robertson, "Leonardo Pisano Fibonacci," University of St. Andrews, October 1998. www-groups.dcs.st-and.ac.uk/~history/Mathematicians/Fibonacci.html.

"The Peasant's Life," Ragz-International, 2001. http://ragz-international.com/peasant.htm.

Francesco di Balduccio Pegolotti, "The Road to China: A Merchant's Guide," Houghton Mifflin College, http://college.hmco.com/history/west/mosaic/chapter9/source273.html.

Gerhard Rempel, "Guilds and Commerce," Western New England College. http://mars.acnet.wnec.edu/~grempel/courses/wc1/lectures/24guilds.html.

Stephen E. Sachs, "The 'Countinghouse Theory' and the Medieval Revival of Arithmetic," May 25, 2000. www.stevesachs.com/papers/paper_90a.html.

Paul Schulz, "The Hanseatic League (Hansa)," GAFA—German American Fellowship Association of MN, April 2001. www.gafa.org/published_articles/21-Hanseatic_League/hanseatic_league.htm.

"Second Council of Lyons—1274," All Catholic Church Ecumenical Councils. www.piar.hu/councils/ecum14.htm.

Société de l'Oriflamme, "Jacques Coeur," XENOPHON Group, June 17, 2002. ww.xenophongroup.com/montjoie/j_coeur.htm.

Patty Strassmann, "The Influence of Spice Trade on the Age of Discovery," About.com, http://historymedren.about.com/gi/dynamic/offsite.htm?site=http%3A%2F%2Fmarauder.millersv.edu%2F%7Ecolumbus%2Fpapers%2Fstrass-1.html.

Jacob Strieder, "Chapter 10—The Fuggers," Bunker Consulting Group, 1999. www.bunkerco.com/masters/chap10.

INDEX

PICTURE CREDITS

Cover Image: © Giraudon/Art Resource, NY

© Alinari/Art Resource, NY, 84

© Archivo Iconografico, S.A./CORBIS, 33, 43, 56

© Bettmann/CORBIS, 91, 93

© Christie's Images/CORBIS, 70

Dover Publications, Inc., 10

© Giraudon/Art Resource, NY, 17, 38, 71, 77

© Historical Picture Archives/CORBIS, 21, 83

© Hulton-Deutsch Collection/CORBIS, 25, 67

Library of Congress, 13

© Mary Evans Picture Library, 37, 52, 90

© Francis G. Mayer/CORBIS, 29

North Wind Picture Archives, 12, 64

© Gianni Dagli Orti/CORBIS, 31, 55, 59

© Scala/Art Resource, NY, 45, 74, 80, 86

© Snark/Art Resource, NY, 48

© Stapleton Collection/CORBIS, 41, 61

© Gustavo Tomsich/CORBIS, 50

Steve Zmina, 16

ABOUT THE AUTHOR

Stuart A. Kallen is the author of more than 170 nonfiction books for children and young adults. He has written on topics ranging from the theory of relativity to the history of rock and roll. In addition, he has written award-winning children's videos and television scripts. In his spare time, Kallen is a singer/songwriter/ guitarist in San Diego, California.